Start
your day
right

Start your day right

Prayer Handbook

Volume 1

Dexter Skepple

Contents

FOREWORD

Prayer is essential in the life of the believer. We all must understand just how powerful it can be, how it can change the course of our lives and empower us to do great things! The bible says that "men ought always to pray and not to faint".

Knowing the power of prayer and believing in the power of it as well, Pastor Dexter Skepple, Pastor of Speak The Word Ministries located in the United States Virgin Islands, began "Start Your Day Right." It was more than a prayer line –it actually was a prayer conference. Pastor Skepple announced this prayer conference to his congregation, posted it on the website (startyourdayright.org) and was ecstatic because he realized that people no longer would have to gather at the church for prayer, they could pray from wherever it was convenient for them, be it standing in their living room, driving to work, taking their children to school, on their knees or standing with their hands upraised, but the exciting thing was that everybody could gather at one time with one purpose and that was to reach heaven as we all communicated with God. Pastor Skepple had a desire to see people's lives transformed.

Start Your Day Right began on October 15, 2012, Pastor Dexter Skepple along with his wife Pastor Terry Skepple prayed and believed God for people who had begun calling from around the world. It was so exciting to see people with a hunger for God and a willingness to pray, consistently calling Monday-Friday 6:30am-6:45am. Since that first day up until now, a year later 54,000 calls have come into the start your day right prayer line (407) 308-0002 and people's lives have been changed.

Eventually a Prayer Team was formulated to include Pastors Dexter and Terry Skepple, Pastor Julie Rhymer, Pastor Malcolm and Teresita Harris, Elders Vicente and Brenda Cotto, Pastor Gerald McDonald, Pastor Celeste Cuffy.

This book of prayer, which can also be downloaded on the website, is a compilation of many of the prayers and powerful confessions that have been prayed and spoken over the last year. With this limited edition *Start Your Day Right Prayer Book* you will be able to pray these prayers and allow the anointing of these prayers and declarations to minister to your heart, change your life, the life of your family, community, country and nation.

For more information about this book, call us at (340) 778-1575 or visit our website at startyourdayright.org or write us at P.O. Box 8304, Christiansted, VI 00823.

Let us pray!!!

THE POWER OF PRAYER

Mark 11:24

Therefore I tell you, whatever you ask in prayer, believe that you have received it, and it will be yours.

Philippians 4:6-7

Do not be anxious about anything, but in everything by prayer and supplication with thanksgiving let your requests be made known to God. And the peace of God, which surpasses all understanding, will guard your hearts and your minds in Christ Jesus.

James 5:16

Therefore, confess your sins to one another and pray for one another, that you may be healed. The prayer of a righteous person has great power as it is working.

1 John 3:22

And whatever we ask we receive from him, because we keep his commandments and do what pleases him.

1 John 5:14-15

And this is the confidence that we have toward him, that if we ask anything according to his will he hears us. And if we know that he hears us in whatever we ask, we know that we have the requests that we have asked of him.

John 15:7

If you abide in me, and my words abide in you, ask whatever you wish, and it will be done for you.

Jeremiah 29:11-15

For I know the plans I have for you, declares the Lord, plans for welfare and not for evil, to give you a future and a hope. Then you will call upon me and come and pray to me, and I will hear you. You will seek me and find me, when you seek me with all your heart.

John 14:13-14

Whatever you ask in my name, this I will do, that the Father may be glorified in the Son. If you ask me anything in my name, I will do it.

1 Timothy 2:5

For there is one God, and there is one mediator between God and men, the man Christ Jesus,

Ephesians 6:18

Praying at all times in the Spirit, with all prayer and supplication. To that end keep alert with all perseverance, making supplication for all the saints,

4

1 John 5:14

And this is the confidence that we have toward him, that if we ask anything according to his will he hears us.

Matthew 21:21-22

And Jesus answered them, "Truly, I say to you, if you have faith and do not doubt, you will not only do what has been done to the fig tree, but even if you say to this mountain, 'Be taken up and thrown into the sea,' it will happen. And whatever you ask in prayer, you will receive, if you have faith."

Matthew 6:9-13

Pray then like this: "Our Father in heaven, hallowed be your name. Your kingdom come, your will be done, on earth as it is in heaven. Give us this day our daily bread, and forgive us our debts, as we also have forgiven our debtors. And lead us not into temptation, but deliver us from evil.

James 1:6

But let him ask in faith, with no doubting, for the one who doubts is like a wave of the sea that is driven and tossed by the wind

1 Timothy 2:8

I desire then that in every place the men should pray, lifting holy hands without anger or quarreling;

Matthew 6:7-8

"And when you pray, do not heap up empty phrases as the Gentiles do, for they think that they will be heard for their many words. Do not be like them, for your Father knows what you need before you ask him.

Acts 12:5

So Peter was kept in prison, but earnest prayer for him was made to God by the church.

Luke 11:9

And I tell you, ask, and it will be given to you; seek, and you will find; knock, and it will be opened to you.

Luke 18:1-8

And he told them a parable to the effect that they ought always to pray and not lose heart. He said, "In a certain city there was a judge who neither feared God nor respected man. And there was a widow in that city who kept coming to him and saying, 'Give me justice against my adversary.' For a while he refused, but afterward he said to himself, 'Though I neither fear God nor respect man, yet because this widow keeps bothering me, I will give her justice, so that she will not beat me down by her continual coming.'" ...

1 John 1:9

If we confess our sins, he is faithful and just to forgive us our sins and to cleanse us from all unrighteousness.

1 Thessalonians 5:17

Pray without ceasing,

Jeremiah 33:3

Call to me and I will answer you, and will tell you great and hidden things that you have not known.

James 5:13-14

Is anyone among you suffering? Let him pray. Is anyone cheerful? Let him sing praise. Is anyone among you sick? Let him call for the elders of the church, and let them pray over him, anointing him with oil in the name of the Lord.

Isaiah 41:10

Fear not, for I am with you; be not dismayed, for I am your God; I will strengthen you, I will help you, I will uphold you with my righteous right hand.

1 Thessalonians 5:16-18

Rejoice always, pray without ceasing, give thanks in all circumstances; for this is the will of God in Christ Jesus for you.

Psalm 141:2

Let my prayer be counted as incense before you, and the lifting up of my hands as the evening sacrifice!

James 4:3

You ask and do not receive, because you ask wrongly.

Romans 10:17

So faith comes from hearing, and hearing through the word of Christ.

James 1:5-7

If any of you lacks wisdom, let him ask God, who gives generously to all without reproach, and it will be given him. But let him ask in faith, with no doubting, for the one who doubts is like a wave of the sea that is driven and tossed by the wind. For that person must not suppose that he will receive anything from the Lord;

1 Corinthians 1:4

I give thanks to my God always for you because of the grace of God that was given you in Christ Jesus,

1 John 5:15

And if we know that he hears us in whatever we ask, we know that we have the requests that we have asked of him

ACKNOWLEDGING GOD FOR HIS NAMES

Father I thank you for being a good God and a loving God. Thank you for caring for me even more than I care for myself. I give you praise and I give you glory for what you have already done in my life. Father I thank you for giving me the permission to come to your throne room boldly and I thank you for what you are going to do today.

I thank you that I can call you Elohim, you are a God of power and might. You are the Lord who is the God Creator. You create blessings for me, you create pathways for me and you cause me to be fruitful over the works of your hands. Father on this day I call you Adonai our Sovereign Lord, you are in all and you fill all and I give you lordship over my life today in the name of Jesus. give you the authority Father to live and abide on the inside of me in the name of Jesus. I submit and surrender completely in all areas of my life to you, I you are ruler and king over me. I thank you Father for being Jehova Rohi, you are the Lord my Shepherd who leads me and guides me and protects me from every hurt, harm and danger seen and unseen in the name of Jesus. Your are there for me when I am in my darkest hour, so I have no fear for you take out of darkness and into your marvelous light of victory. I thank you Father for being Jehova Shammah, The God who is ever present, I thank you that I can feel your presence right now in the name of Jesus. I thank you that everywhere I go you are with me. Father I come before you and I lift up my hands to you as I call on you as Jehova Tsidkenu the Lord my Righteousness, I am not righteous by my own merits but you have declared me to be righteous and I thank you that today I can declare that I am the righteousness of God in Christ Jesus. Thank you Father that this day you would lead me in the path of righteousness in the name of Jesus. I thank you for being Jehova Jireh and for providing for me. I thank you Father for supernatural provision and I thank you that that provision comes to me from the north, from the south, from the east and from the west. Father I receive you today as my provider and my source in the name of Jesus. You rebuke the devourer for my sake that I may be a delightsome land. You are my multiplier who increases me and my household more and more. I thank you Father for being Jehova Nissi, my banner and my protection. Father I thank you that when the enemy comes in one way you cause him to flee from before me in a thousand different ways in the name of Jesus. You said in your word that when the enemy comes in like a flood you Spirit raise up a standard against him. I thank you Father that your word says in Psalm 91 that a thousand may fall at my side and ten thousand at my right hand but it will not come near me in the name of Jesus.

I thank you for releasing your anointing over my life. I thank you that no evil shall befall me neither shall any plague come nigh my dwelling in the name of Jesus. Father I give notice to every spirit that would try to attack my mind, my soul, my spirit that would try to tear me down. I plead the blood of Jesus from the crown of my head to the soles of my feet. I thank you that you are Jehova Rapha and your healing anointing is available to me. Father today I declare that by your stripes I am already healed. I am totally healed and totally blessed in the name of Jesus. Cover me under your wings, fill me with your spirit and your anointing in the name of Jesus.

Father I come against the spirit of Depression and Oppression and I declare that you have no power, no authority and no rights to be in my mind. I cancel your assignment against me now in the name of Jesus. I receive the joy that is unspeakable and full of glory for I am at God's right hand where there are pleasures evermore. I cancel the spirit of Death, and I do not receive it, instead I receive the spirit of Life and life more abundantly in the name of Jesus.

I thank you and I worship you for what you have already done in the spirit. Father as I go about my daily work, I receive your word and I in graft myself in your word. Father your word says let the redeemed of the Lord say so, and I say that I have been redeemed from the hand of the enemy and from the curse of the law and I say it has no power and no authority in the name of Jesus. Father I declare it and decree it to be so in the precious, anointed name of Jesus Amen.

BLESS THE LORD FOR HIS GOODNESS AT ALL TIMES

Father I thank you and I approach Your throne of grace acknowledging that You are a good God, You are an awesome God. I thank You for what You have already done in my life. Father, teach me how to chase after you daily, and seek your presence. Father I release the anointing and the presence of the Holy Spirit everywhere that I go in the name of Jesus. Father I also ask that Your presence and anointing follow me throughout the day in the name of Jesus. I declare that something good is going to happen today because You awaken me with praise on my lips. You said in Your word in psalm 23, that goodness and mercy will follow me all the days of my life. I thank You that Your favor surrounds me and is in me in the name of Jesus. Father You said in Your word that if we acknowledge You then you would direct our path, so I come to You this day knowing and acknowledging that You are a good God. I wait on You to lead me, guide me and direct me in all my ways the name of Jesus. I thank you Lord that your angels are encamped around me. Father I don't expect man to protect me, though I do thank you for Law Enforcement officers, however I know that You are my Source and my Protector. I am under your divine protection and I thank you for that in the name of Jesus. Lord I thank You that You said in Your word, taste and see that the Lord is good. I have tasted and I have seen that you are a good God. I thank You that You would open up doors for me today that were previously closed in the name of Jesus. Things that were shut up to me, Father I thank you that they open to me today in the name of Jesus. Father I ask that you lead me to someone today that has not known you as their Lord and personal Savior. May I share the Lord Jesus Christ with them not only with my lips but also through my leadership and life style. Allow me to pray for them and lead them into the things of God.

Father, everything that the enemy brings my way I render it powerless, ineffective to operate against me in the name of Jesus. Satan your power is broken and you have no authority over my life in the name of Jesus. Father I thank You that whatever the enemy means for bad, you turn it around for my good. Lord I thank you that as your child I do hearken to Your voice and the voice of the stranger I do not follow. I thank you Father that when the enemy begins to speak to me, you have the authority to pull down and cast out every wicked and every lawless imagination that comes against my mind in the name of Jesus. Father I pull down and render ineffective these wicked imaginations to work against me in the name of Jesus. I thank you that the strongman does not have a strong hold over my life nor does he have any dominion over my life in the name of Jesus.

Father I thank you once again for what you have already done in my life and I give you all the praise and all the glory in Jesus name Amen.

COME BOLDLY TO HIS THRONE OF GRACE TO OBTAIN HELP

Father I come before Your throne of grace speaking what you have spoken, declaring what You have ordained from the foundation of the world. Father it is my covenant right to come before You and to declare the very oracles of God over my life. Father I am here to magnify you and lift You up and to say that You are a good God and an awesome God. Thank You for being Jehova Jireh, my Provider and I want you to know just how much I love you, honor you and praise you. Father I thank you that I am satisfied with you and you alone. I rejoice to know that our help is in the name of the Lord who never sleeps nor slumber but is the keeper of my soul. I thank you that in my weakness you are made strong. It's not by my power or by my might but by your Spirit.

Father I know that we are strong in you and in the power of your might and where two or three come touching and agreeing, there you will be. I also know that we wrestle not against flesh and blood but against principalities, against powers, against rulers of darkness this world and against the spiritual wickedness in high places. Father I thank you that you have given us as a body of believers as well as individually, the authority to pull down strongholds over churches, over our lives, over countries, over nations and I come touching and agreeing with other believers nationwide and around the world. We come into covenant and in agreement with you concerning our lives and our destinies. We know that our destinies and our lives are in your hands and not in ours. We release the will of God over lives today in the name of Jesus. Father we shut out negative words, thoughts, and we pull it down in the name of Jesus. We cancel negative thoughts against our minds, against our spirits and against our souls in the name of Jesus. We cast down thoughts of despair, we come against the spirit of suicide and depression that would come into our minds and cancel out the word of God in our lives. Father today we pray over our mouths, that you would guard our mouths, help us to guard our tongues that we may no longer be angry or dismissive in the name of Jesus. We release the anointing of God over our lives and Father we thank you that you are able to do supernaturally, exceedingly, abundantly above all we could ever ask or think in the name of Jesus. Father I thank you that when the enemy comes in one way he will flee from before us in seven different ways. Father we pray that your will be done over our churches and we cancel that assignment of the enemy against our marriages, our children, relationships and we plead the blood of Jesus over these areas. We thank you that you would cause us to run and not be weary. We thank you that we have the spirit of the finisher and we can overcome every obstacle that comes our way in

16

the name of Jesus. We thank you that from the crown of our heads to the sole of our feet the anointing of the Holy Spirit rest over us and you cause us to triumph in every area of our lives. As we go our separate ways and do what you have called us to do we ask that you guide us and lead us. May the meditation of our hearts be acceptable to you. We ask that you perfect those things which concerns us. Father we give you praise and we give you glory for what you have already done in and through our live in Jesus' precious name Amen.

PRAYER FOR FAVOR AND DIVINE CONNECTIONS

Father I thank you for this day, I rejoice in you for this is Favor Day. I thank you Father, I trust you and I believe in you. I thank you that my mind is alert and my body is strong and I am well able to do what you have called me to do today in the name of Jesus. . Father I thank you for divine connections today. Thank you for leading me to people that I may be connected with those whom you have assigned for me in the name of Jesus. Father I ask that you give me good positive people that I can align myself and be connected with in the name of Jesus. People who have great influence in the market place, people of godly wisdom, integrity and authority in the name of Jesus. God I thank you that my divine connections are a step in advancing into my destiny. It is a step in progressively moving forward your kingdom. I thank you Father that just as the branches are connected to the Vine and those branches are able to produce much fruit, I thank you that I am primarily connected to you. My fruits will show others my divine connection with you as it did with

PRAYER FOR FAVOR AND
DIVINE CONNECTIONS

Joseph in Potiphar's house. The fruit of wisdom, favor and prosperity will draw those divine connections that you have ordained for me like a magnet in the name of Jesus. Father with the blood of Jesus I come against every negative connection that I may have and I ask that you destroy those connections now in the name of Jesus. Father remove all evil companionships and people with evil intentions, motives and agendas in the name of Jesus.

I thank you that your favor is extended to me everywhere that I go. People will watch me and declare favor over me. Father I thank you for your favor over businesses and that favor flows now over business minded men and women. Father I thank you that as a business owner I have your favor and you have blessed me with prosperity like never before in the name of Jesus. I thank you Father that in the midst of financial turmoil, you are not only in it with me, but your divine favor and prosperity covers and shelters me from the turmoil. I thank you that my business will attract people. People will be blessed by my business so I thank you for the anointing to prosper and bless others in the name of Jesus. Father I pull down every stronghold and I plead the blood of Jesus and I say that I am blessed. Father help me to uplift your name in everything I do and everything I say for I am yours and I am called by your name. I thank you for divine favor and prosperity over me. I thank you that my destiny rests in your hands, thank you for leading me, guiding me and giving me supernatural wisdom. You are the one that tells me what to do, how to do and where to go. Father I thank you that every time I open my mouth something begins to happen, things are being released in the atmosphere. Help me to always remember that I frame my world with the words that come out of my mouth.

Help me to guard my mouth because the words I speak have life. So I declare that I will only speak your word in the name of Jesus. I declare that what I speak is what I will have, so let your anointing rest on me, let your favor cover me and go before me, let my hands prosper in everything that I set them to, and let my feet be guided to the divine connections that you have foreordained for me, in Jesus name I pray Amen.

PRAYER FOR PEACE OVER OUR ISLAND, SCHOOLS AND FAMILIES

Father I thank you that on this day my heart is opened and receptive to your word. I recognize my need for you and how that I cannot do anything without you, and I cannot make it without you. Father as I go through this day I acknowledge and I recognize that you are God and you are Lord over my life.

Father I pray this day against the spirit of violence that has rested over our island even on our nations. Father I pray against this spirit that is bringing disruption is operating over the people, Father I break its hold in the name of Jesus. Father every person that is carrying a weapon with a malicious spirit, I come against that spirit and I break it now in the name of Jesus. I declare that we are a people of unity that love you and trust you. We put our islands in your hand, we put our nation in your hands and Father I break that spirit now in the name of Jesus for we recognize that you are the Lord our Peace. So by your word let our island and our nation be covered in your peace and everyone with weapons in their hands with the intent to do harm, cause them to drop it in the name of Jesus. Let them Lord, sense your presence in such a way that they would turn from the wickedness of violence and turn to you Father in repentance in the name of Jesus. Every spirit of strife, confusion, desperation, contention, abuse, suicide, murder, thievery, and every demonic, wicked and evil spirit attached to violence; I bind it and I cast them into the pit of destruction now in the name of Jesus. By the power of the blood of Jesus, I break the curse of violence on our island and over our nation and I declare let your peace that passeth all understanding flow like a mighty river now in the name of Jesus. Let your joy that is unspeakable and full glory with your unconditional love fill the hearts of the people of our island and our nations now in the name of Jesus.

Father I pray now over the educational system beginning with teachers. Give each teacher a heart like yours. Give each teacher wisdom, on how to do, what to do, and where to go. Give them wisdom on what is the best way to communicate with students and give them innovative ideas on how to help the students learn in the name of Jesus. I thank you God that you cause teachers to rise up to their call and to walk worthy of their call and their vocation in the name of Jesus. Father as students go to school today I pray that there will be peace in the schools today. Let that peace that rest in our homes follow each child into their schools in the name of Jesus. I submit everything to you concerning students, teachers and the entire school system in the name of Jesus. Father, cause students and teachers alike, to hear your voice and the voice of the stranger let them not to follow. Father cause us to be willing and yielded vessels as we listen to your voice. Any person who has rejected your voice Father, this day I declare that they will hear and obey and they no longer will be people who reject you.

Father, I pray for marriages and that there is no division within any of our marriages. I thank you that there is unity as you said Lord, that where there is unity there is strength. I declare that over our marriages that they are strong, our families are strong and are serving you. I thank you that the hearts of the fathers and mothers are returning back to you, the hearts of the children are being turned back to you in the name of Jesus. Father we reverence and respect the sanctity of marriage and I speak over marriages that the enemy is trying to destroy, Father I speak peace it now in the name of Jesus. The spirit of anger that may be resting over the husband and the spirit of unforgiveness that may be over the wife, I come against it now in the name of Jesus. Father I bombard the heavens and I pull down every stronghold by the power of your word that are over marriages now in the name of Jesus. Father you said that if your people who are called by your name would humble themselves and pray, turn from our wicked ways then you would hear us and heal the land. Father I thank you that we are people who know how to wait on you, even as you said in the book of Isaiah, that they that wait upon the Lord shall renew their strength, they will mount up as eagles, they will run and not be weary, they walk and not faint. Help us to be people that can wait on you and not be moved by every wind blows against us, nor by what others may say about us. We are people who are rooted and ground on your word. Father help us in the time of making important decisions to wait and hear your voice before we move in the name of Jesus.

Father I thank you today for release your perfect peace over our island, our nations and in our homes. Thank you for showing yourself as our Shepherd who leads us and guide us and as our Lord who is Peace in Jesus name Amen.

PRAYER FOR SINGLE PARENTS AND PURPOSELESSNESS

Father I thank you for the opportunity to lift up your name and place our request before your throne of grace. I just want to thank you for all that you are and everything that you have done for us because we do not take it for granted. I come to you with a grateful heart and I set you above every circumstance that we may be facing and so I call on you as Adonai the Sovereign Lord. You always have everything under control so I acknowledge you as the God that has everything in our lives under control. I declare Lord God that I believe in you and I put my trust in you with all my heart. I leave nothing covered or hidden from you and I come to you and I open my heart and life to you. I uncover everything before you and I ask oh God that you search me, try me and know the ways that are in me that is not of me. Father me on the right path and on the way that is everlasting.

I lift up before you this morning single parent homes. I thank you for every single father and single mothers who are raising their children/child alone. Thank you Father God for blessing them with supernatural strength and for placing people around them who would support and encourage them in what they are doing. I pray Father God that you would give them the wisdom they need and bless them with favor. You said in your word that the blessing of the Lord it maketh rich and addeth no sorrow with it. I come against every demonic spirit of weariness or feelings of being overwhelmed but strengthen them in you and in the power of your might. May you uphold them in your right hand of righteousness. I come against every spirit of fear and I thank you that there is no fear in their hearts but bless them to know what to do and how to do regarding their children and their children's future. I pray that you would give them the knowledge to know how to speak to their children.

I pray for those who feel purposeless not knowing what they are suppose to do and feeling depressed because of that; Father I lift those people up to you today. I thank you that you would speak to their hearts and first of all let them know that you are with them. I thank you that you would have them to know that if you are with them then you are more than the world against them. I thank you God that your word says that you have great plans for us, your plans are plans of good and not of evil to give us a future and a hope God in the name of Jesus. Thank you Lord that you have foreordained a destiny for us and that you will reveal it to them even now Lord in the name of Jesus. I thank you that they will fulfill their destiny, purpose, vision and mission that you have assigned to them. Thank you for placing a man and woman of God that will lead them into their divine purpose and destiny in the name of Jesus. Those of us who are struggling to believe in your goodness even as we follow the path to our purpose and destiny, help them to believe in your goodness in the land of the living. Help them to know that your goodness and mercy follows them everywhere that they go in the name of Jesus. I thank you that this day will be a great day, a day of great expectations for us all in Jesus name Amen.

PRAYER OF SURRENDER

Father I thank you for the anointing that is present and available to me in the name of Jesus. Father I thank you that the fervent effectual prayers of the righteous avails much. Father I surrender all to you today. Father I thank you that your mercy endures forever and that you have taught us through your word that we can boldly come before your throne of grace and obtain mercy. I thank you Father that I am able to obtain mercy in the name of Jesus. Father, allow me to experience your goodness and mercy today in the name of Jesus. Father I lift holy hands to you today and I lift up my heart before you because you are well able to do what no one else can do. Father I put you ahead of everything and everyone in my life today in the name of Jesus. Father I declare you to be the center of my life and there is nothing that can compare or be in competition with you in the name of Jesus. Father I acknowledge that you are an awesome God and that your presence dwells inside of me. I thank you that you would take me, lead me and guide me. I choose to follow you. Father your word says in Proverbs 3 that if I acknowledge you then you would direct my path. Father I acknowledge you today and I am putting you first, I am putting you ahead of every situation and circumstance in the name of Jesus. I thank you that you would surround me today with people of wisdom. Release Father the wisdom of the Holy Spirit over my life in the name of Jesus. I submit myself to you Father that you may correct me and minister to me all through the day. Father I put on the altar my sins, hurts, habits that does not come from you. I surrender them all to you now in the name of Jesus. I thank you for your provision today. You are a supernatural God and you are able to provide for me in the name of Jesus. I thank you that there is supernatural provision available to me today. Father I surrender all my financial problems to you today in the name of Jesus. I thank you that you will send provision from the north, the south, the east and from the west. I thank you Father that you have allowed us to receive your supernatural provision in the name of Jesus. I declare that there is an open door over my life in the name of Jesus. I declare that the windows of heaven are open to me in the name of Jesus and the Holy Spirit is pouring out blessings over my life today like never before. I thank you Father that you are Jehova Shalom, the God of Peace, help me to sense your peace in the midst of turmoil. I declare that I have strength and I will not faint in the day of trouble. I thank the Holy Spirit for releasing that strength over my life in the name of Jesus. I surrender my body to you today and I declare that there is total healing over my life in the name of Jesus. I am healed from the crown of my head to the soul of my feet and healing virtues of God flows through my body in the name of Jesus.

I come against every demonic spirit that has been assigned to me to destroy me. Father your word declares that no weapon that is formed against me is able to prosper and every tongue that rises against me shall and will be condemned in the name of Jesus. I cancel the assignment of the enemy against my family/relationship/marriage, my finances, my health and I render it useless and ineffective against me in the name of Jesus. I thank you Father that sin has no dominion over my life and the life I live, I live in and through Christ in the name of Jesus. Father I thank you that there is no fear in my life, I dismiss the spirit of fear. You did not give me a spirit of fear but have given me a spirit of faith and I release faith over my life in the name of Jesus. I give you praise and I give you glory for what you have already said and declared over my life in Jesus name I pray Amen.

PRAYER TO BREAK ADDICTIONS

Father I thank you for this day and I rest in the assurance of your word for my life. Father your word says to trust in you. I declare that I will trust in you and lean not unto my own understanding. Father you said to acknowledge you in all our ways and you would direct our path. Father today, I acknowledge you as my Source, my Strong tower and my God. Father I pray the prayer of Jabez over my life today. Father bless me indeed on this day and enlarge my coast; enlarge my territory. Let your hand be upon me, keep me from harm that I may be free from pain. I declare that I am blessed exceedingly, abundantly, above all that I could ever ask or think. Father I declare that your anointing rest over me. Father I thank you that even when I go though I am going through a storm you protect me and you call me blessed.

Father I pray for those who are struggling with addictions. I thank you yokes are being destroyed as I pray and bondages are being destroyed because I serve the yoke destroying, bondage breaking God in the name of Jesus. Father I thank you that you said in your word, is there anything to hard for God? I thank you that no addiction is too hard for you. You are the God that makes the impossible, possible. I come against those addictions now in the name of Jesus and I plead the blood of Jesus against it. I declare that they are whole, there is nothing broken and nothing missing in the name of Jesus. Father you said that what we say is what we will have if we believe it. So I believe and receive that as I pray there is an anointing to break addictions, an anointing to break habits that are hard to break in the name of Jesus. Father I declare you to be a habit breaking God and you are breaking every bad habit now in the name of Jesus. Father I believe that it is already done, I don't have to see it to believe it, I know that it is so and it is done in the name of Jesus.

Father I pray for families who may have lost a loved one because of an addiction. I thank you that you are a present help in the time of trouble and so help them to surrender every hurt over to you. Father there are some things that we do not understand so I place those things in your hands for you are a loving and caring God. Father I pray your peace that passes all understanding over those families, let it rest in their hearts and in their minds today. Father I thank you that as I lift them up in prayer that they can sense your strength and your anointing rising up on the inside of them like never before in the name of Jesus. Father I thank you that those families are healed, those who arestruggling with addictions and habits are struggling no more, I declare by your word that they are free and whom the Son sets free is free indeed, in Jesus name Amen.

PRAYER FOR PROTECTION FOR THE DAY

Heavenly Father, I thank You that You are an awesome God. I thank You, Lord Jesus, that You have declared over my life that I will live a long and healthy life. I thank You for being my Bread of Life and for releasing Your strong and mighty angels over my home, in the name of Jesus. I thank You, Father, that You are my dwelling place. In You I dwell and in You I have more than enough, in the name of Jesus. I thank You, Father, that when I need a friend You become that Friend that no one else can be to me. I can speak to You and I can pour out my heart to You, knowing that when I speak to You, You hear me and it stays with You. I thank You that Your anointing is with me and that You are my Shield and Buckler, my Comforter, my Chief Cornerstone, my Deliverer, and the Horn of My Salvation, in the name of Jesus.

Father, I thank You that the words of my mouth and the meditation of my heart are acceptable to You this day, in the name of Jesus. I thank You that You would make the crooked things straight and the rough areas smooth. As I go out on my daily activities, I pray that You would protect me from every hurt, harm, and danger. I plead the blood of Jesus over my life, and I declare that no weapon that is formed against me is able to prosper. Father, I thank You that You go before me and prepare the way for me. Thank You for being my shelter and fortress, for You said that the righteous run in and they are saved. Thank You that the assignment of the enemy against me is cancelled and made powerless in every way, in the name of Jesus. I thank You that when the enemy comes against me one way You cause him to flee in seven different ways. When the enemy comes in like flood, Father, You are Jehova Nissi, my standard and my banner that is lifted up against him. When the enemy sets traps and snares against me, Lord, I thank You that he is ensnared and it is he who falls in the very same trap. I thank You that You drive the enemy away from me like the chaff is driven by the wind. I thank You that You contend with those that contend with me, and You cause them to walk in dark and slippery places with the angel of the Lord afflicting them. Father, I thank You that I can dwell safely under Your wings. No evil shall befall me, for I am in the palm of Your hand. You said in Your word that the enemy should touch not Your anointed, so Father, I thank You that I will not be afraid of the terror by night, nor of the arrows that fly by day, nor of the pestilence that walks at noon day. I thank You that You have given Your angels charge over me to keep me in all my ways. Father, I thank You that this day You will show Yourself to me as my Protector and my Stronghold, in Jesus name. Amen.

PRAYER FOR HUMILITY AND RIGHTEOUSNESS

God of wonders, You are holy and I stand in awe of Your majesty. Father, I ask that Your divine provision would fall upon me on this day, in the name of Jesus. Thank You for my daily bread that You provide, Lord, in the name of Jesus.

Father, I pray today for a spirit of humility. Lord, help me to humble myself under Your mighty hand, that in Your good timing, in due season, I shall be exalted. Lord, I come against the spirit of pride, and I take authority over it, for You said in Your word that You hate pride. So, Father, I pull down pride, haughtiness, vanity, and every spirit associated with pride, in the name of Jesus. Father, continually allow me to humble myself, to go on my knees with my hands lifted as a sign of humility and surrender. I thank You that Your word said that when pride comes so does emptiness and shame but with the humble comes skillful, godly wisdom, so I receive Your skillful and godly wisdom and I reject pride, in the name of Jesus. Father, I make a decision today to be of a humble spirit that I may receive the reward of the humble. Father have Your way in my life like never before, in the name of Jesus.

Father, you are a righteous God; rest a spirit of righteousness on me and put on me the robe of righteousness. Father, I acknowledge that I am the righteousness of God in Christ Jesus. Father, I pray that You would give me a hunger for Your righteousness as I humble myself to You. Give me, oh God, a hunger for Your word, a hunger and a thirst for You. As David said, Lord, like a deer pants for the water brook, so let me thirst after You and Your righteousness that all things would be added to me. Father, I thank You that I will study Your word, for it is in Your word that I will receive divine revelation, in the name of Jesus. I thank You that Your will is to be done in and through my life. Father, I thank You that my desires are in alignment with Yours. What You want for my life is what I desire, in the name of Jesus. Father, I ask that You would destroy any stubbornness, rebellion, and disobedience over my life, in the name of Jesus. Every hindrance, obstacle, and stumbling block that is in my way, Father, cause it to be removed now, in the name of Jesus. Father, I thank You that You make every crooked thing straight and that the footsteps of a righteous man are ordered by You. Father, lead me and guide me on the path of righteousness. Your word said that blessed are those who hunger for righteousness, who are persecuted for righteousness sake. Father, I thank You that I am blessed because my desire is for Your righteousness that I may stand strong in the day of persecution. Father, I thank You for being everything I need in my life; thank You that Your spirit of humility rests on me and I am clothed in your righteousness, in Jesus name. Amen.

PRAYER TO COMMAND YOUR MORNING

Father, I come before Your throne of grace and I give You the honor and all the praise; I acknowledge You as my Lord and Savior. You are the Creator of all. I thank You for the privilege to be alive and for all my senses at work and that I am well. Father, I thank You that this is the day that You have made and I choose to rejoice and be glad in it.

Lord King, I pray that every move I make today and every word that flows out of my lips will bring praise, glory, and honor to Your name. May I be approved by You today, Father. Lord God, I ask for your Spirit over my life and corporately over Your body. Father, Your word says that we can have what we say, and You are not a man that You should lie nor the son of man that You should repent. You said that when a king declares a thing it will be established, so I command and take authority over my day, in the name of Jesus. I speak that every blessing that You have aligned for me and every benefit that You have loaded me up with shall and will be reaped, in the name of Jesus. Father, I thank You that my destiny and my purpose will cooperate with everything that You have aligned for me today. Father, I say that today I press toward the mark in Christ Jesus. Anyone or anything assigned to frustrate or undermine or hinder or even hurt or harm me in anyway, I command it to be removed from my sphere of influence, in Jesus name. I declare that it cannot stand in the name of Jesus. I greet with great anticipation all the good things that You have prepared for me. I bless my ministries, my job; I bless my businesses. I declare that a new day has dawned on me in my finances, in my relationship, in my health, in the name of Jesus. I ask for the presence of the Holy Spirit in my life today. I download Your success, Your health, Your prosperity, Your vision, Your direction, Your ingenuity, Your creativity, Your holiness, Your righteousness, Your peace, and Your resources into my day, in the name of Jesus. I declare that I am victorious. Lead me today, Father God; give me Your grace, patience, and meekness that everyone I come in contact with may see the fruit of the Spirit activated in my life like never before, in the name of Jesus. May Your light shine in me brightly today, Father; let your glory come forth, Father, so others can come into the glory of your splendor, Father. I thank You for refreshed excitement, a fresh zeal, and a fresh anointing. Father, I am in hopeful expectation of Your miracles, of Your signs and Your wonders. I decree and declare that something good is going to happen today.

Father, under this anointing I declare that anything diabolical is repelled and it is inoperative and ineffective against me, in Jesus name. I plead Your precious blood over my household, Father, over my ministry, my job, my business, in the mighty name of Jesus.

PRAYER TO COMMAND YOUR MORNING

Father, grant me kingdom asylum and diplomatic immunity from any evil that seeks to imprison me or entrap me. There are evil spirits that seek to work against me today, Father, but I declare that all my assignments and activities will be pure and holy before You, in the name of Jesus. I ask that You would assign Your angels as divine escorts and supernatural security, Father. Let all evil devices be exposed, in Jesus name. Let my enemies be at peace with me, in the name of Jesus.

Let a spirit of productivity and excellence shine forth today, in Jesus name. Let everything that the enemy made crooked be made straight by the power of Your Holy Name, Father. Thank You for victory, I receive Your victory, in Jesus name. Holy Spirit, thank You for guiding me into all truth; order my footsteps today. Almighty God, bless the works of my hands, provide advancement, promotions, wisdom, knowledge, visions, investments, dreams, multimillion dollars ideas, in the name of Jesus. I speak inventions and strategies. I declare that settlements, profits, bonuses will come forth to me, in the name of Jesus. Let there be unexpected financial blessings, and let the hidden riches of secret places come forth, in the name of Jesus. I speak that Your kingdom power would rest over me. Let Your kingdom come and Your will be done on earth as it is in heaven, in Jesus name. Amen.

PRAYER IN CHOOSING GOVERNMENT LEADERS

Father, I thank You, I honor You, and I bless Your Holy Name. I thank You that You are our God and we are Your people. I thank You that You are the true and living God and there is no other God but You, Lord. I thank You for who You are; You are the King of kings and the Lord of lords. You are the Beginning and the End, You are Holy, You are our Deliverer, You are our Strong Tower, and You are our Healer. I thank You for this day, for this is the day that the Lord has made and we will rejoice and be glad in it. You are our Father; we can come boldly and declare that You are our God.

Lord, I bless You today and I declare today that You are God over this land. Father, I thank You as I go to the polls to elect government officials; I thank You for the privilege to be able to do so. I declare that You have already set men and women of wisdom, character, honor, and faith. I thank You that they are men and women of understanding, peace, and courage. I thank You for Your word that says when the righteous are in authority the people rejoice. Father, I thank You that because the righteous will be set in authority, there will be change, change for Your honor and glory. Father, I thank You for peace and protection while we go out to the polls. You said in Your word that blessed is the nation that calls you Lord. Father, I ask that just as You chose David because of his heart, that You would choose through us the men and women who are after Your heart. I pray that they shall govern and lead our nation, our country, with wisdom and understanding.

Father, in the name of Jesus, I take authority over the strongman, the principalities and rulers of darkness of this world and the spiritual wickedness in the high places that would try to influence the leaders of the land. In the name of Jesus I bind and rebuke spirits of greed, corruption, injustice, bribery, blackmail, character assassinations, racketeering, money laundering, extortion, confusion, strife, contentions, pride, selfishness, gain, and any other demonic, wicked, and evil spirit. I render ineffective, powerless, useless, null and void every wicked imagination, every high minded thought, close mindedness, limited thinking, favoritism, lack of vision, lack of insight and direction, demonic plots, schemes, agendas, ploys, and plans of the devil against our leaders, in the name of Jesus. I release over the leaders of the land righteousness, truth, unity, peace, protection, a just and wise mindset, big thinking, vision, direction, focus, diligence, integrity, mental and physical strength, compassion, understanding, knowledge, good stewardship, and justice, in the name of Jesus. Father, I thank You that You are the one who sets one up and takes them down, so I trust You and I am confident that the men and women whom You have already chosen will govern under the control of the Holy Spirit and our land will be at peace and in prosperity, in Jesus name. Amen.

PRAYER OF WARFARE

Father, in the name of Jesus, I thank You for being Jehovah Gibbor, the God who makes war. Thank you for being Jehovah Saboath, the Lord of hosts. You are the Lord strong and mighty in battle. This day, Lord, I thank You for Your presence and for Your anointing. I thank You for Your grace and for Your power that is available to us. . I thank You God for being a good God and for Your mercy that endures forever. Father, Your word says to put on the full armor of God that I may be able to withstand the attacks of the devil. You also said to be strong in the Lord and in the power of His might. Father, I put on the full armor of God and of light. I clothe myself in the Lord Jesus Christ. I thank You that You teach my fingers to fight and my hands to do war. I thank You that You have given me the strength to bend the bow of bronze which is an act of war in judgment against the enemy. I thank You that You said in Your word that You have given me power and authority to tread upon the scorpions and the serpents and over all the power of the enemy and nothing by any means will hurt me. I thank You, Father, that You would clothe Yourself in Your garments of war and You contend with those who contend with me; You fight against those who fight against me. So I say to You, Father, lift up Your spear and the javelin and close up the way of those who pursue me. Let the angelic host excel in strength as I release Your word against the enemy as a double edged sword. Let the angel of the Lord surround me and keep me and my household as I lift up my voice in prayer. Father, I thank You in the name of Jesus for what you will do this day.

Now, Father, You said in Your word that we do not wrestle against flesh and blood but against principalities, against powers, against rulers of darkness of this world and the spiritual wickedness in the high places. You also said that the weapons of our warfare are not carnal but they are mighty through God for the pulling down of strongholds, casting down every wicked imagination and every high thing that would lift itself up against the knowledge of God. I pull down every stronghold that the enemy would use against me to kill, steal, or destroy. Every negative thought, every wicked and lawless imagination I take authority over and I cast down, I reject them now, in the name of Jesus. Every feeling of bitterness, unforgiveness, rejection, anger, fear, depression, and oppression and in every area of my heart and soul that the enemy would try to use against me to destroy me and my God given destiny, I turn over into the hand of the Master, and I receive Your delivering power now, in the name of Jesus.

Satan, the blood of Jesus is against you and you have no part, no place, and no authority over my life to destroy it, in the name of Jesus.

God, I thank You for giving me the authority to bind and loose, and I bind every lawless spirit; every sexually immoral spirit; witchcraft spirits; spirits of fear and depression; spirits of suicide, lukewarmness, spiritual laziness; spirits of confusion, contention, and strife; spirits of lack, affliction, and poverty; spirits of sickness, disease, weaknesses, and infirmity, and I thank You, Lord Jesus, that they have no power and no authority to rule against me, in the name of Jesus. Father, even as Your word says to let my enemies walk in dark and slippery places, let the angel of the Lord drive them like the chaff is driven in the wind. Father, let every negative word that is spoken against me be returned to them seven fold, in the name of Jesus. I cancel and make null, void, empty, powerless, useless, inoperative, and ineffective every negative word that is spoken against me and my household. Let the plans, plots, ploys, assignments, and agendas of the enemy against me and my household be aborted and die, in the name of Jesus.

Satan, I say to you to release me and let me go, in the name of Jesus.

Father, I violently attack the spiritual darkness over this land and over this country. I tear down and pull down the wickedness in the high places over this land and my country. By the power of the blood and the name of Jesus let them be destroyed and consumed by Holy fire. I thank You that you are already turning things around for our good and Your glory, in the name of Jesus.

Father, You said that death and life are in the power of my tongue, so I declare supernatural increase to follow me everywhere that I go. God, I thank You that You have brought me into my wealthy place. Father, I pray for increase, and I thank You that Your word says that it is Your will for me to prosper and increase, my household and me more and more. I thank You, Father, for the way you will lead me and guide me; You brought me out of poverty and lack and every demonic hold that the enemy would have against me. God, I declare Your favor to follow me like never before, in the name of Jesus.

Satan, your power is broken and you have no authority over my life. As a child of God I release you from your assignment against me, and I thank my God that by the stripes of Jesus Christ I am healed and I am whole.

I thank You, Father, that my mind is sound, I have no fear, I have the joy of the Lord. I thank You, God, for bringing me to where I am now and for where You are taking me, in the name of Jesus. Thank You, God, for bringing me into my divine destiny; I am destined to win and You cause me to triumph in every area of my life, in the name of Jesus. Father, I give You praise and I give You glory for what You have done already in the spirit realm over my life, in the name of Jesus. God, I am mindful to give You and You alone all the glory, all honor, all the adoration, all the thanksgiving for what You are going to do in my life. I declare that I have the victory. Victory belongs to me in the precious and matchless name of Jesus. Amen

PRAYER OF THANKS FOR THE BLOOD OF JESUS

Father, I thank You for anointing me this day like never before. Father, today I submit myself under Your mighty hands; I thank You for Your authority and the way You wrap me in Your arms. I thank You that You protect me and cover me with Your precious blood.

Father, Your word says that there is life in the blood, and I thank You for the shed blood of Jesus over my life, in the name of Jesus. Today I activate the power of the blood of Jesus over every area of my life. Father, I thank You that it is through Your blood that I have been made righteous and justified, for You took on my sins and nailed them to the cross. By the power of Your blood I am freed from all sickness and disease that may try to come upon my body. Every illegal movement of the enemy against my body now ceases by the power of the blood of Jesus. Everything now becomes whole, healed, and well, in the name of Jesus. By the power of the blood I declare that my household is saved and sealed until the day of redemption. Father, according to Your word Jesus has destroyed the power of sin over my life because of the shed blood, so I thank You that I am dead to sin and alive in Christ. Sin has no dominion over me, and by the power of the blood of Jesus I thank You that my body is now the temple of the Holy Spirit. I thank You that it is because I am covered in the blood of Jesus that You remember my sins no more, for they are as far from me as the east is from the west.

Father, I thank You that it is by the blood of Jesus Christ that all generational, familial, and ancestral curses are destroyed. By the blood of Jesus strongholds and wicked imaginations are destroyed. By the blood of Jesus every demonic attack against me is cancelled and made inoperative, in the name of Jesus. I thank You that in and through the blood of Jesus, You place walls of protection around me and my household, and the enemy dares not cross that bloodline, in the name of Jesus.

Father, I thank You for the blood of Jesus Christ. I thank You that Your blood makes me whole, that it has allowed me to be able to access all the promises of God, and that it has allowed me to be seated with You in the high places. I thank You that by Your blood I can enter into the kingdom of heaven; I have been redeemed, restored, renewed, justified; and I am able to have a relationship with You. Father, I thank You for the precious blood of Jesus Christ over my life. Amen.

WHEN THE ENEMY COMES IN LIKE A FLOOD

Father, I thank You this day that You are my help in times of trouble. Father, Your word says that our help is in the name of the Lord. I thank You that You are my Shelter in the midst of the storm and You are my bridge over troubled water. You are my Peace in the midst of the storm, and I thank You for covering me under Your mighty wings.

Father, You said in Your word that when the enemy comes in like a flood the Spirit of the Lord will raise up a standard against him. Father, I thank You that the trials, situations, circumstances, and tribulations that I am going through are but for a season. I thank You that this, too, shall pass and I am being led up, out, and into my wealthy place. Father, I thank You that I can count it all joy, for my faith is being strengthened. I lean on You, Lord, and not unto my own understanding, and in all my ways I will acknowledge you. I thank You that as I face difficulties, the Holy Spirit becomes my Guide and Comforter through it. I thank You that in this time of trouble I can say that all is well and trouble does not last always. Father, I thank You that You said in Your word to fear not for You are with me and that I should be of good courage, so I thank You that You are my Hiding Place and my Strong Tower which I can run into and be safe.

Father, I thank You that no weapon that is formed against me is able to prosper, so I declare that by the blood of Jesus every weapon that has been formed is utterly destroyed now, in the name of Jesus. I take authority over distress, stress, anxiety, worry, doubt, restlessness, negative situations, circumstances, trials, tribulations, hindrances, afflictions, obstacles, snares, and traps of the enemy, in the name of Jesus. I declare that these weapons are made null and void, useless and inoperative, ineffective and powerless against me in every which way, in the name of Jesus. Father, contend with those who contend with me and cause the enemy to scatter in seven different ways, in the name of Jesus. I declare that everything that the enemy meant for harm, You have turned around for my good and for Your glory, in the name of Jesus. I declare that I choose to rejoice at all times, and I change mourning for dancing and a spirit of sorrow for a spirit of gladness. I declare and decree that the enemy is under my feet and I trample on him according to Luke 10:19. I thank You, Lord, that your warring angels are encamped around me and they keep me. My mind is stayed on You, so I declare that I have Your perfect peace that passes all understanding.

Father, I thank You that this is the day that You have made and I will rejoice and be glad in it, and I will bless You at all times, knowing that if You are for me, who can be against me? I thank You that I am an overcomer, and You cause me to triumph. I declare that victory is mine and this is my day of breakthrough. Father, I thank You and I bless You for being my way-maker, bondage breaker, and yoke destroyer; thank You for being my freedom and my peace, in Jesus name. Amen.

PRAYER FOR WISDOM

Father, I thank You today that You are a good and awesome God. I am thankful that Your mercy endures forever and I acknowledge You as the Omniscient God, the All knowing God who is Wisdom.

Father, today I ask for Your divine wisdom. You said in Your word that if any man lacks wisdom to ask it of You without wavering, for You give wisdom freely. So Father, I ask today that Your skillful wisdom rests over me. I thank You that I have the mind of Christ and Your wisdom is formed within me. Father, You said in Your word that wisdom is the principle thing and that with all my getting I should get understanding. Father, I thank You that as I search and study Your word I receive Your wisdom. I thank You that in and through Your wisdom You will lead me, guide me, and order my footsteps. I thank You that I will rightly discern between right and wrong that I may know what to do and how to do, what to say and when to say. I thank You that Your wisdom rests on my mind and flows from my lips as a fountain of living water, and those who receive of it would cherish it as choice silver. Father, You said in Your word that I should attend to Your words and forget not my benefits. I thank You that because I walk in Your divine wisdom I enjoy the benefits of joy, peace, health, and healing. I thank You that You cause the works of my hands to be blessed and those blessings come without sorrow. Father, I thank You that throughout this day You will place people of wisdom around me to pour into my life that of the abundance I receive I may pour it out on someone else.

Father, I take authority over the spirits of confusion, lost concentration, distraction, uncertainty, doubt, idle thinking and speaking, negative thinking, and any other evil spirit that might try to attack me in the area of wisdom. I declare them to be defeated and inoperative, in the name of Jesus; and I function each and every day in the knowledge and the wisdom of Him who created me. My mind is alert and my ears are attentive to the divine wisdom of God. I declare that I do not walk in the counsel of the ungodly, and I let no corrupt communication come into my ears or proceed out of my mouth. I thank You, Father, that I speak words that are in due season and that Your wisdom that comes forth is a blessing to the hearer for building up. Father, I thank You this day that I will operate in the fullness of Your wisdom, knowledge, understanding, and counsel, and I thank You that your anointing to flow in Your skillful wisdom rests on me today and everyday, in Jesus name. Amen.

PRAYER FOR DISCERNMENT AND TO BRING SOULS INTO THE KINGDOM

Father, I thank You for this day and I acknowledge You as an awesome God; You are a mighty God. I thank You that You would stretch forth Your hands over me today as I pray, in the name of Jesus. I thank You that You hold me in the palm of Your hand, and I thank You that You have numbered the hairs on my head. Thank You for loving me the way that You do, and I thank You for what You are doing in and through my life. I pray that You will open up the windows of Heaven and pour out such a blessing that I don't even have enough room to receive it.

Father, I pray for a spirit of discernment that I may know what You are saying and what You are doing, in the name of Jesus. Father, I declare that this is my season and this is my time. I thank You that according to the book of Isaiah that I have the tongue of the learned and I know how to speak a word in season. I thank You that because I have the tongue of the learned I know what to say and when to say it when I open my mouth. Father, I ask that You fill my mouth with the wisdom of Your word. I thank You that I would come to know You better as a result of studying Your word, believing Your word, and filling myself up with Your promises. Father, I thank You that all the promises that You have made to me will be fulfilled, in the name of Jesus. As You have spoken, Father, I thank You that not one of Your words concerning me will be empty or go unfulfilled, in the name of Jesus. Father, Your word is truth and You cannot lie, so every promise that You have given me I declare will come forth, in the name of Jesus.

I pray that You would give me a spirit of Boldness. Allow me to speak Your word with boldness. I will not be timid and I will not be ashamed of the gospel of Jesus Christ, for it is power and it is life. I pray for unbelievers that You may receive them today; everyone who does not believe Your word or has rejected Your word, I declare that Your anointing would rest over them, even as I pray in the name of Jesus. Father, Your word says that it is by the Holy Spirit that men are convicted, so Holy Spirit, I ask even now that You convict the hearts of the unbelievers that You will lead me to today. I ask that You replace the heart of stone with a heart of flesh that it may be good grounds to receive the word of the Lord, in the name of Jesus. God, You said in Your word that I should let your light shine before me that they may see Your good works and glorify my heavenly Father who is in heaven. Father, I pray that my work on this day will bring glory to Your name. I thank You that unbelievers who come around me feel the love of Jesus and would throw up their hands in surrender, wanting to receive the Lord Jesus Christ as their Savior. I declare that they are saved, delivered, set free, and made whole, in the name of Jesus. God, I thank You today for allowing me to lead souls into Your kingdom. Thank You that You think through me and speak through me and this will be a fruitful day for me, in Jesus name I pray. Amen.

PRAYER FOR HEALING FOR LOVED ONES

Heavenly Father, I thank You for being such an awesome God, and I thank You that in You there are no limits. Thank You, Father, for being my bread of life, for when I need to be fed and sustained You feed me. Thank You for allowing Your Sprit to rule and control my mind, my heart, and my life. Father, I eliminate the work of the devil in my life and I turn my life over to You; I surrender all to You, in the name of Jesus. Father, thank You for being my shield and my buckler, for shielding my life and preventing the enemy from destroying, hurting, or harming my life, in the name of Jesus. Father, thank You for being my Comforter, so that in times of sorrow You comfort me. Thank You for allowing the Holy Spirit to come into the areas where there is sadness or sorrow that He may comfort me, in the name of Jesus. Thank You, Father, for being my Cornerstone and my Deliverer; You are the one that delivers me from every sickness, disease, and sin. I thank You that You delivered me by the power of the blood of Jesus. Thank You, Father, for being my Dwelling Place; in You there is life and there is no death. I thank You, Father, for releasing Your Spirit and Your anointing over me this morning. I thank You that You have called me to be in You. You said in Your word that if any man be in Christ he is a new creature. The old things have passed away and behold all things have become new, in the name of Jesus. Father, I thank You that You are my Fortress. When the enemy sends his flood or his demons against us, I thank You that the Spirit of the Lord will raise up the standard against him. I thank You that even if others desert me, You are a friend that sticks closer than a brother. I thank You that You are someone that I can speak to and that can minister to me. Thank You, Lord, for being the Almighty God and for sitting on the throne of my life. You are Lord of all. Thank You that You would lead me and guide me this day, in the name of Jesus. Thank You for being the Horn of my Salvation.

Father, I lift up those who struggling with sickness and disease in their bodies. Father, I declare that healing belongs to them, in the name of Jesus. You said that by Your stripes they are healed. I stand in agreement with them, in the name of Jesus. Father, I cancel the assignment of the enemy to operate against us, to pull us down. I declare that no weapon that is formed against those who are suffering is able to prosper, and so I declare that this weapon of sickness and disease is completely destroyed, in the name of Jesus. Every disease and sickness that touches their bodies dies instantly, in the name of Jesus. I thank You, Father, that You will show Yourself to be Jehovah Rapha, the Lord our Healer. Let Your angels minister to their bodies and bring swift healing in this hour, Lord, in the name of Jesus. Father, I thank You that our children have the mind of Christ; thank You that there is healing and it begins with our children as they go to school, Father. I ask that You cover them from the crowns of their heads to the soles of their feet. I speak prophetically that things are turning around and that help is not just on its way but it is already here, in the name of Jesus.

Father, I stand in agreement with Your word that we believe the report of the Lord that they are healed, they are whole, and there is nothing broken and nothing missing, in Jesus name. I thank You that it is never over until You say that it is over, Father, so I prophesy that all is well, in the name of Jesus. Amen.

BORN WITH FAVOR PRAYER

Father God, I thank You that this is a day of miracles; this is the day that You have made; I will rejoice and be glad in it. I thank You and I know that nothing happens by coincidence, but Father, You have a plan and a blueprint for my life. Father, I live by that blueprint, so I ask that You show and expose to me my part in that blueprint, in the name of Jesus. I thank You that Your plans for me are plans of good and not of evil. I am always on your mind, so I know that my life is perfectly planned by You. Father, I thank You that no weapon formed against me shall prosper and every tongue that rises against me shall be condemned. I thank You that You established me in righteousness and oppression is far from me. I take the sword of the Spirit and I use it now against my enemies; I overcome everything because greater is He that is in me than he that is in the world.

Lord, I bless Your Holy Name, and as I prepare to go to the work place and do the things that You have assigned for me to do, I declare that this is a day like no other and I call forth miracles. I speak forth blessings over my household, that everyone in my household is above and not beneath, the head and not the tail. I thank You that we do not operate with a spirit of fear, timidity, cowardice, nervousness, or anxiety, but we walk in power, in Your anointing; we walk in holiness and righteousness. We walk hand in hand with You and in Your miracle working power. I know that if You are for us there can be no one who can stand against us. I do not operate as though this world has any power over me, for I am in this world but I am not of this world. I operate as a kingdom citizen, as a king that is under the King and I am a lord under the Lord. I refuse to commiserate with the enemy, to take suggestions from the enemy, and I refuse to operate as though I will not win, in the name of Jesus. I will not beg, for You said in Your word that You will not see Your children beg for bread. I receive a breakthrough spirit and I do believe for all things are possible. I believe, Father, for other families to be healed, restored, and made well. I believe for husbands and wives to come home, for children who have strayed away to come home now, in the name of Jesus. Thank You, Father, for blessing me with Your favor, and I thank You that that favor overtakes me and my household. Thank You for breaking the bonds of poverty, inferiority, and low self-esteem because I know who I am and whose I am. I thank You that I have been born with purpose and I have been born with favor to complete my divine assignment; I will remain faithful to the end until it is fulfilled, in the name of Jesus. Father, help me to be like Christ in all my interactions with people everywhere that I go. I thank You that they do not see me but they see You in m,e Lord, in the name of Jesus. I thank You that Your Spirit lives within me and I step out with great expectations of what You will do on this day. Father, I thank You that all my provisions for this day come from You and Your peace will abound toward me

61

today. In Jesus name I pray. Amen.

PRAYER FOR FREEDOM FROM BONDAGE OF SIN

Father, I thank You this day that You become my Deliverer, my Bondage Breaker, and my Yoke Destroyer. You are my freedom and I thank You that You are my Light and my Salvation.

Lord, I ask Your divine forgiveness of my sins: hidden sins, unconfessed sins, sins of the past, sins done in my heart, Lord, every besetting sin that is in my life, known and unknown. You said that a broken and a contrite spirit You will not turn away, that You will forgive my sins and remember them no more. Father, forgive me for the sin of that I have allowed to take dominion over me. Father, by the power of Your blood and by the power of the name of Jesus free me from this captivity. Today I make a decision to die to the old man and sin; I make a decision to crucify the flesh with all its cravings and complete surrender to the Lord Jesus. I declare I die now to sin and am alive in Christ Jesus, and the life I now live, I live it hidden in Christ. I declare that now there is no condemnation to me, for I am in Christ; I am a new creature and His workmanship.

Father, in the name of Jesus, You have given me power and authority over the enemy and his demonic forces and You said in Your word that for this reason was the son of man, made manifest to destroy the works of the devil, to set the captives free, and preach liberty to the prisoners. Father, by the power of the blood of Jesus, let every unholy, demonic, satanic, and wicked soul tie that I have formed be consumed in the fire of the Holy Spirit. I declare that any residual feelings, emotions, thoughts, longings, desires from the soul tie are completely destroyed, in the name of Jesus. I reject, rebuke, refuse, and dismiss everything and anything associated with the soul tie. Father, every ungodly and unholy attachment to the world and corrupt companionships, unequal yokes, bondages, and strongholds of the mind and spirit, shackles, fetters, chains, snares, and cords that seek to destroy me, let them be destroyed and come to nothing now, in the name of Jesus. Father, I declare that the power of the enemy over my life, sin, destruction, and death are cancelled, made inoperative, useless, powerless, and ineffective against me in every area in my life now, in the name of Jesus. Father, any words that have been spoken against me to keep me in bondage to sin and the devil, I declare them to fall dead to the ground and I impose the word of God which is of a greater authority over my life, and I declare that I will live and not die and declare the works of the Lord.

Father, I thank You that I am set free, I have received the truth of Your word, and I receive my freedom now, in the name of Jesus. I have been redeemed, I have been delivered, and I am free and whom the Son sets free is free indeed. Father, cause my heart, spirit, soul, and body be attached to You. Cause my soul to be tied and knit to You in love, and bind me to You in the cords of love and reconciliation. Father, thank You for my freedom, in Jesus name. Amen.

PRAYER FOR THOSE WHO HAVE STRAYED AWAY

Father, I thank You this day, for You are a good and merciful God. You are full of loving kindness, and I thank You that You never leave us and You never forsake us. Father, I thank You for Your word that says that You are married to the backslider and that You love us beyond our faults.

Father, I ask for those who have strayed from Your divine will for their lives. Father, I pray and declare over their lives that You would manifest Yourself in their lives that they may know that You never leave them, but You are with them always. I thank You that they are always on Your mind and it is why You send godly men and women to them to encourage them in their walk with the Lord. Father, You said that the plans You have for them are plans of good and not of evil, that You have begun a good work in them and You are faithful to complete it. Father, I thank You that in the midst of turmoil and confusion that You would shine the light of Your glory brightly that they may find their way back to You. I thank You for the Holy Spirit

PRAYER FOR THOSE WHO HAVE
STRAYED AWAY

who is the one that convicts the hearts of men and brings them to comfort of Your loving arms. So I declare that wherever they are and whatever they are doing, may they sense the tugging and wooing of the Spirit; may He be so insistent that they cannot ignore Him. May the Spirit be so vivid to them that they run to the church and make amends with You, Lord, that they go back on the path of righteousness. Father, I thank You that even the struggles and hardships that they are currently experiencing will serve as a means to drive them back into the fold. Father, I pray that from the time they enter into the house of God or surrender to You at their bedside or any other place in which brokenness has entered their hearts that they may cease from a wicked way. Lord, may they sense Your love, peace, and forgiveness toward them. May they accept what You freely give to them and be set free, in the name of Jesus. Father, You said that You can turn the hearts of men any way You choose, so I thank You that not only have You turned their hearts toward You but that You have changed the heart of stone for a heart of flesh.

Now Father, You said that death and life are in the power of the tongue and that we can have what we say if we believe when we pray. So Father, I speak over them what You have already spoken about them that they are Your workmanship created in Christ Jesus. I declare that they are dead to sin and are alive in Christ and they belong to Your household. I declare that they are Your royal priesthood, and that they walk in works that You have predestined for them. I declare that their footsteps are ordered of You, for they are Your sheep and the sheep of Your pasture. I declare that they hear Your voice and the voice of the stranger they will not follow. I declare that now there is no condemnation to them, for they are in

67

Christ and they are new creatures; the old has passed away and behold, the new has come.

Lord, I come against condemnation, guilt, shame, unforgiveness, bitterness, false feelings of burdens, frustrations, self hatred, rejection, and any other demonic spirit that would keep them from Your grace. I take authority over these spirits and I cast them into the pit of destruction and by the authority of the name of Jesus I claim those souls that have strayed away from the mastership of Jesus. I plead the blood of Jesus over their minds, and I ask that the Balm of Gilead flows over every open wound in their souls to restore and refresh them, in the name of Jesus.

Father, I thank You, that today by the power of Your spoken word every backslider, every person who has strayed away returns like the prodigal son, in the name of Jesus. I declare that we shall see sons, daughters, husbands, wives, relatives, and friends return to You, Lord, that we may celebrate victory over the enemy, in the name of Jesus. Father, I thank You for extending Your hand of love, mercy, and grace over all of us, in Jesus name. Amen.

PRAYER WHEN YOU ARE IN COURT

Father, I thank You for this day, thank You for life and life more abundantly. This is the day that You have made and I will rejoice and be glad in it. Father, I thank You that today You would show Yourself to me as my Shield and the Horn of my Salvation. I thank You that You are my Prince of Peace, my Shelter, and my Fortress.

Father, today, as I enter into the court house, I ask that You go before me and prepare the way for me. I ask, Father, that You become my Advocate and my Defense. Father, You said in Your word that no weapon that is formed against me shall prosper and every tongue that rises against me shall be condemned. Father, evil men have risen their tongues in false witness against me; I ask, Father, that You expose the truth in the midst of lies. I ask, Father, that even as I stand before the Judge today, that he and those around him may see a spirit of excellence in me. I ask that You give wisdom to my attorney, give him/her a sharp mind and alert ears to hear the lie in order to come against it with the truth. Father, You said in

Your word to put on the full armor of God that I may be able to stand; so I put on the armor and I gird myself with the belt of truth. You, Lord, are the Truth, the Way, and the Life, so Lord, by your grace which is sufficient, I declare I will stand at peace knowing that in my tongue flows the absolute truth.

Father, in advance I come against miscommunications, misinterpretations, character assassinations, stigmas, lies, false witnesses, unjust rulings, intimidation and manipulation, and any other spirit that would try to discredit me and my character, by the power of the blood of Jesus. I declare that their lying tongues will be divided, for You said they should touch not Your anointed and do Your prophets no harm. I declare that they shall be ensnared by the words of their mouths, that they will be tangled up in the idle words that they speak and their lies will be exposed, in the name of Jesus. I plead the blood of Jesus over the Judge that he may hear the truth and rule justly, over the jury that they may hear and discern rightly, and over my attorney that he/she may defend me with the wisdom and knowledge that comes from You, Lord.

Father, I thank You that even as You showed up on behalf of Daniel in the lion's den and on behalf of his three friends in the fiery furnace, I thank You that You will shut the mouth of the enemy and be that fourth man with me that everyone may know that I serve the God of Truth and Justice. Father, I thank You that You hold me up in Your right hand of righteousness so I need not fear what man may say against me. If You are for me who can be against me? Thank you, Lord, for being my Light and my Salvation. You are my Captain in charge and the One who fights against those who fight against me. I declare that today victory is mine and all the glory, the honor, the praise, and the thanksgiving go to You, Lord God, in Jesus name. Amen.

PRAYER FOR DAILY STRENGTH

Father, I thank You that You are my Strong Tower, my Fortress, and my God in whom I trust. Father, I acknowledge You this day as a good and gracious God, a God that loves unconditionally and a God whose mercy endures forever.

Father, I come to You this day seeking Your strength. Father, You said in Your word to be strong in You and in the power of Your might. Father, I yield to Your supernatural strength this day; I surrender everything that I strive and struggle with to You, Lord. I declare and receive what Your word says: "Come unto me all who are heavy with burden and I will give you rest." Father, I cast all my burdens and all my cares upon you and in exchange I receive Your rest. I thank You, Father, that even as I wait on You to provide me with the answers I need for the situations that I face, You will renew my strength like the strength of an eagle. When I am feeling disappointed or sad, I thank You that Your joy becomes my strength. Father, I thank You that even when I am hard at work doing Your labor of love, I will not be weary in well doing. Father, I ask for spiritual strengthening so that I may be able to stand against the wiles of the devil and against his host, for I wrestle not against flesh and blood. I ask for strength in areas of my soul that I may not walk according to the flesh but only be led of Your Spirit. Give me the strength, Holy Spirit of God, not to speak anything corrupt, not to partake in ungodly conversations, and help me not to react to a negative situation based on my emotions but rather based on the Spirit of God. I ask for strength in my physical body. Lord, You said that when I am weak You are made strong. Father, allow Your strength to be poured over me as I do my daily work that I may be able to accomplish my tasks for the day.

Father, I come against tiredness of spirit and body, weariness, laziness, strife, contention, frustration, false burdens, oppression, depression, heaviness, worry, and any other spirit that would try to rob me of my strength. Father, I bind these spirits and I cast them down to the pit of destruction, in the name of Jesus. I declare that no weapon formed against me will prosper and I will stand strong in You, Lord, and in the power of Your might. I plead the blood of Jesus over every area of my life in where I may be weak and I declare myself to be strong, in the name of Jesus.

Father, I thank You that with Your strength comes peace and rest. Father, I cease now from all my doings to rest in Your perfect peace. I thank You that You are my burden bearer and I can cast all my cares upon You for You care for me and You know what I go through. I thank You that I can confidently trust and lean upon You. Thank You for being my Shelter, my resting place, and my exceeding joy, in Jesus name. Amen.

PRAYER TO BE SPIRITUALLY DRESSED FOR THE DAY

Father, I thank You that You are my Divine Covering and You shelter me under Your wings. I thank You that You are my great and exceeding reward and Father, I bless Your name. I say that from the rising of the sun to the going down of the same Your name is worthy to be praised. I acknowledge You today in all my ways and I ask that You would perfect those things that concern me.

Father, this day I ask that You would dress me in the garments that You have prepared for me that as I go out I may be recognized as a son/daughter of God. Father, I ask first of all that You cleanse my heart, Lord God, that the intentions and motives of my heart may be acceptable to You. Wash me and cleanse my mind and my spirit by the washing of your word, that my mind may only dwell on things that are pure, perfect, lovely, and of a good report. Father, I thank You that I will clothe my mind in the mind of Christ and Your wisdom is formed in me. I thank You that for an undergarment I put on the garments of Salvation, for You have saved me from the

PRAYER TO BE SPIRITUALLY DRESSED
FOR THE DAY

wages of sin and have brought my spirit alive through Christ Jesus. I put on, also, the garments of Praise, that there may be a new song in my heart and a praise on my lips, for You have been good to me and You have been everything that I needed You to be. So in praise, I lift my voice giving You thanks, glory, and honor. I put on the robe of righteousness, for You have made me to be in right standing with You through the shedding of the blood of Jesus on Calvary's cross. You have made me to be in right relationship with You by removing sin and the old man. I put on over my priestly garments the full armor of God. I put on the breastplate of righteousness which guards my heart against the corrupt way of thinking and doing of this world. I put on the belt of truth, for You are the Way, the Truth, and the Life, and knowing the truth of Your word is what sets us free from the cares of this world. I put on the shoes of the preparation of the gospel of peace. In the midst of turmoil, negative circumstances, trials, tribulations, strife, contentious situations, obstacles, and hindrances, I thank You that I can walk in Your peace that passes all understanding and that peace rests and rules in my heart. I take up the shield of faith that quenches the fiery darts of the wicked one, and I lift up the sword of the Spirit which is the word of God. Father, I thank You that as I speak Your word in faith, by your word every crooked thing is now made straight. I put on the helmet of salvation, which keeps my mind stayed on You and my thoughts acceptable in Your sight. Father, above the armor I clothe myself in the Lord Jesus Christ. May He be seen and heard through me. I decrease that He may increase in me. May the very nature and attitude of Christ be seen and heard as I go into the world. May those whom You have assigned to me today sense the very presence of God that they may know that I was sent by You to reach out, uplift, encourage, strengthen, and bring those people into Your fold.

Now, Father, I thank You that I am fully dressed, and I thank You, Holy Spirit, that You would anoint my head with the oil of gladness; may Your miracle working power rest on me this day, in Jesus name. Amen.

PRAYER FOR THE SERVICE

Father, I thank You for being a great and an awesome God. I thank You that You are a God that loves to be in the midst of His people. I thank You for showing Yourself as our Heavenly Father who fills all with Himself.

Father, this day I lift up our church service. I thank You, Father, that You will be glorified in our service today. Father, You said in Your word that You inhabit the praises of Your people, so Father, I lift up the praise and worship portion of our service to You. I thank You, Lord, that You will be high and lifted up and all men will be drawn unto You. I thank you that we can lift up holy hands before a holy God and we can magnify you in song. I thank You, Father, that we will sing a new song, we will shout with the voice of triumph, and we will dance like David danced. I thank You that we will give You praise and You will be exalted as Head above all. We will rejoice in You as we declare the works of Your hands, and I thank You that as we worship You our worship will be a sweet smelling perfume. I thank You that we will pour out our worship on You like spikenard oil, in intimate worship that we may enter into the Holy of Holies where Your angels declare Your glory. Father, I pray that as You are ushered into the service that You would move freely, unhindered, and flow like mighty rivers of living water. May every song that is sung bring pleasure to Your heart; may the melodies played by the musicians minister to You that You can flow in and through the singers and musicians as You set the people free from demonic oppressions, depressions, and spirits of heaviness. Even as David played for Saul and by the anointing the evil spirit on Saul left, I thank You that Your anointing will flow from the praise and worship team to bring healing, joy, deliverance, peace, and Your unconditional love.

Father, I pray for the man and woman of God who will be ministering the word to Your people. I thank You that they have been before Your face seeking wisdom, knowledge, understanding, and counsel for Your people. I thank You that their ears are sharp and alert to hear what thus saith the Lord concerning His plans for His people. I thank You that as they have diligently studied they are not bound to what they have studied but are sensitive to the leading of the Holy Spirit during the service. I thank You that they will flow and minister completely under the control of the Holy Spirit that everyone may know that You are a God that speaks and reaches out to His people through His servants. I thank You that the word that they bring is a life changing word, a word that would impact, encourage, uplift, discipline, and correct the children of the house. I thank You that it will be a word that brings conviction of sin to the unbeliever and the backslider, a word that would bring light into their darkness, to set them free from the works of darkness. I thank You for their salvation in advance, in the name of Jesus.

PRAYER FOR THE SERVICE

Father, I pray for the deacons, elders, ministers, intercessors, altar call workers, and every other ministry leader that is involved in making the service a success. I pray that Your anointing would rest on them that they may minister under the power of the Holy Spirit, under the divine wisdom of God, and with the love of God in all mercy and spiritual understanding.

Father, I come against the works of darkness, principalities, spiritual wickedness, satanic and demonic forces that would try to lift themselves up against our service. Father, let every scheme, plan, ploy, plot, agenda, and snare come to nothing and fail. I plead the blood of Jesus over the man and woman of God who will bring the word, the praise and worship team, and over every other area of the service and ministry. I declare that warring angels are released to fight on our behalf and form walls of protection around us, in the name of Jesus.

Father, I thank You that souls will be saved, delivered, and set free by the resurrection power of Christ. I thank You that You will pour out an uncommon anointing over our service where we will sense the presence and power of God like never before. I thank You that what we do in the service will be attested with signs, wonders, miracles, supernatural deliverance, and supernatural breakthroughs. I thank You for the victory in advance and I give you all the glory, all the praise, and all the honor, in Jesus name. Amen.

PRAYER WHEN SEEKING EMPLOYMENT

Father, I thank You this day for being the God who is my Source and my Provider. I thank You that You are the Creator God who creates a blessing for me and Your favor goes before me that all may be well in my life.

Father, this day as I go out looking for employment, I thank You, Lord, that You will bless me with a spirit of excellence and wisdom. I thank You that You would clothe me with both meekness and boldness. I thank You, dear Lord, that You would lead me and guide me to the right place and speak to the right person concerning employment. I thank You, Lord, that my character and my work ethic will be my witnesses concerning the quality of an employee that I am. I thank You, Lord, that You order my footsteps today and Your presence is with me everywhere that I go. Father, I thank You that those who look upon my employment application and my resume would know instantly that I am the person for that job. I thank You that through this job my needs would be met and I will lack for no good thing. I thank You, Father, that even as the employer considers me, Father, that he/she will sense Your presence concerning me and I will be chosen about everyone else. You said that I would be the head and not the tail, so I thank You that You have given the necessary skills and talent that set me apart from everyone and that the employer may see me as an asset to the company in every area, in the name of Jesus. I thank You, Lord, that my gifts and talents make room for me and Your favor rests on me and goes before me. I thank You, Lord, that everything that You have in store for me is now being released to me, in the name of Jesus.

Father, I take authority over fear, anxiety, doubt, low-self esteem, disappointments, discouragements, and any other spirits that would try to destroy or sabotage what I set out to do. I plead the blood of Jesus against these spirits, and I declare that no weapon formed against me shall prosper. I declare that this is my day of triumph, this is my day to step into something greatness, this is my day to begin what God has ordained for my life, in the name of Jesus. God, I thank You in advance for my job. I thank You that You have led me to where You need me to be, and I thank You for providing this job for me that I, too, may be able to give into Your storehouse in tithes and offerings. I thank You, Father, for Your goodness and mercy toward me, in Jesus name. Amen.

PRAYER TO BREAK CURSES

Father, I thank You for this day and the way that You will show Yourself mighty in my life. Thank You that You are Jehovah Gibbor, the Man of War, and Jehovah Sabboath, the Lord of Hosts. You are my Shield and Buckler, and I thank you that you are my Rearguard.

Father, I thank You that the strongman is already bound over my life and is released from his assignment against me. Father, not only is he released but he must return the things that have been stolen, held back, and captive. I receive my freedom from every bondage and every chain, for whom the Son sets free is free indeed. I thank You that I have been redeemed from the curse of the law. I break all curses of lust, perversion, rebellion, poverty, witchcraft, idolatry, rejection, fear, confusion, addictions, death, and destruction, in the name of Jesus. I declare that these things are broken off from my life, in the name of Jesus. This day has been appointed and created for me to be free; I run, break out, and breakthrough, in Jesus' name. I command all generational spirits that came into my life during conception, even in the womb and in the birth canal and through the umbilical cord to be destroyed unto ashes, to never take root and lose all power in my life, in the name of Jesus. I break all spoken curses and negative words that I have spoken over my own life. I make them all of no effect; I speak death to those word and they shall not take root nor live in me, in the name of Jesus. Holy Spirit, release Your fire to burn from my foundations, every debris from the past, all spiritual trees from its roots that have been planted in my life to destroy me, things that have been assigned to hold me back. Let them be burnt to ashes now, in the power of the name of Jesus. Cleanse me, oh Lord, from all hexes, jinxes, spells, incantations, witchcraft prayers, obeah, voodoo, Santeria, satanic oaths; cause them to be destroyed in the power of the blood of Jesus. I command that all ancestral spirits, involvements with free masonry, idolatry and witchcraft, false religions, polygamy, lust, and perversion come out now, in the name of Jesus. Father, I am free and I declare that God's word that is of the highest authority be superimposed over all curse and seeds that have been planted in my life from my youth by the spoken word of those that were around me; I break their power and what was placed over me now, in the name of Jesus. I break all chains and fetters that come with hereditary spirits to be destroyed utterly, in the name of Jesus. I break every legal right that any curse maybe operating under by the power of the blood of Jesus. Curses of sickness, diseases, infirmities, weaknesses - let them be destroyed now and forever by fire and by the blood of Jesus. Father, let every curse that was spoken against me become a blessing, even as Balaam tried to curse Israel yet he could not speak anything but blessings, so let it be with my enemies now Lord, in the name of Jesus. I thank You, Lord, that the more the enemy tries to afflict me, the more I multiply and expand as Israel did in Egypt. I declare that relational curses of adultery, fornication, divorce, division, strife, contentions, rejection, abandonment, neglect, abuse, bitterness, vengeance, and unforgiveness be destroyed completely from their roots, in the name of Jesus.

Father, on this day I walk in spiritual freedom, I walk in supernatural favor, I walk in supernatural victory; all chains, fetter, manacles, yokes, bondages, soul ties, satanic alliances and allegiances, demonic oaths, pacts, and contracts I declare to be null, void, destroyed, and burnt to ashes now, in the power of the blood and the name of Jesus. I thank You that I walk in Your peace, I am under Your wings, Your angels are encamped around me, You are my strong tower, and I am under Your blood. Your firewall surrounds me and I am in your everlasting arms, in Jesus name I pray. Amen.

PRAYER WHEN FEELING WORRIED

Father, I thank You this day for being my Peace. Thank You that You are my Strong Tower and my Burden Bearer.

Father, I come to You, in the precious name of Jesus, that I may cast my cares upon You. Lord, You said in Your word that we should not be anxious for anything, that You know our needs even before we petition You for them, so Father, I thank You that I am always on Your mind and Your eyes are upon me. Father, I thank You that every stronghold of worry, defeat, anxiety, lack of faith and trust, and fear are pulled down, overthrown, and destroyed now, in the name of Jesus. I also release all negative expectations from my mind, all evil foreboding. I command it to be destroyed, pulled out, rooted out, and overthrown, in the name of Jesus. I command all my thoughts to go back under the obedience of Christ. Father, I put my trust in You. My trust is not in man or in things, even as Your word says not to put our trust in chariots or horses but only trust You. Father, You also said in the book of Matthew that we should not worry for what we do not have, or focus on what needs we have but that we should seek You first, Your kingdom, and Your righteousness and all things would be added unto us. I thank You, Father, that I will not fret for what others are doing or saying, but I put my trust in Your holy word which is established. I shall not fear for what will happen in the future, for You will never leave me nor forsake me and Your perfect love casts out all fear. I thank You, Lord, that my confidence in facing negative situation rests on You, You lead me, You guide me, and You are the one who makes crooked places straight.

Father, I declare what You have already declared over my life. You said let my mind be set on things that are above and if my mind is stayed on You, then you would give me perfect peace. You said that I should only dwell on things that are good, lovely, and praiseworthy. You are my help, and my help is in the name of the Lord. You guard me and keep me; therefore, I shall not be moved. I walk by faith and not by sight, for Your word will not return to me empty but it will accomplish what it has been sent to do. I declare that I lean on You, not my own understanding, that Your presence rests on me and in me; therefore, I will not worry about anything that I may be going through. I thank You that the work You began in me You are faithful to complete. I thank You that You perfect those things that concern me; therefore, I will not be moved by the situations that surround me. I declare that Your peace that passes all understanding rests and rules on my heart.

Father, I thank You that I can rest in peace, knowing that all things are in Your control, that everything the enemy meant for bad You turn around for my good and for Your glory. I thank You that

PRAYER WHEN FEELING WORRIED

I have already overcome and I walk in victory, in Jesus name. Amen.

PRAYER TO BREAK GENERATIONAL BONDAGES

Father, I come to You this day thanking You for being the Bondage Breaker and Deliverer over my life.

Father, I come to You today seeking help and freedom from the bondage of generational iniquity, transgression, and sin. Father, You said that the sins of the fathers are visited upon their children to the third and fourth generation. Father, today I recognize the generational iniquities, transgressions, and sins of my father and forefathers, and I stand in the gap for them, myself, and the generations after me. I ask for forgiveness of all inherited, generational, ancestral, and familial transgression, sin and iniquity. I ask that You cleanse and purify my generational line in the blood of Jesus. I declare this day that by the blood of Jesus that covers me and my children that these bondages, curses, limitations, and afflictions that have been passed down through the DNA and bloodline be destroyed and die, in the name of Jesus. I declare that because I am born of the spirit, everything concerning me, my family, and the generations after me are now under the lineage of the Lord Jesus Christ and, therefore, we are inheritors of all the blessings of Abraham. I thank You, Father, that by and through the power of the Holy Spirit everything that has become a stumbling block, hindrance, snare, besetting sin, inherited sin, and generational demon is now destroyed, annihilated, and brought to nothing, in the name of Jesus.

Father, You said that by Your word all things were created, that death and life are in the power of the tongue and they that indulge in it will eat the fruit thereof. Father, I speak death and destruction to these generational, ancestral, familial, and inherited iniquities, sins, and transgressions. I speak death to come swiftly to root of it and may there be no evidence that it ever existed, in the name of Jesus. I declare that my generations after me are blessed spiritually, emotionally, psychologically, and physically, in the name of Jesus. Diseases, infirmities, weakness, disabilities, character sins, sexually immoral sins, mentally disturbing and mentally binding demons, torments, tendencies, habits, attitudes, mindsets, past failures, disappointments, and everything else that is attached with the old generational bloodline now dies and is of no effect to me and my generations after me, in the name of Jesus. Now I speak life to the generational line after me; let every blessing, dream, achievement, gift, talent, resource, innovative idea, monies, and everything associated with the will of God for my generational line, live and come to pass in my life and the lives of my children, in the name of Jesus. I declare that whatever was buried with the old generations that was to be brought about be resurrected and be accomplished, in the name of Jesus. I declare that my bloodline and the bloodline of the generations after me is cleansed, blessed, and anointed to prosper.

Father, I thank You for freedom for me and my generational line. I thank You that we walk in liberty and we are empowered to succeed, progress, and move forward, in Jesus name. Amen.

PRAYER TO RELEASE THE ANGELIC HOST

Father, I thank You today for the privilege and honor to stand in Your presence. I declare You to be the Lord of Host, the King of Glory, and the King of the angels. I thank You, Father, that You are a very present help in times of need.

Father, I thank You that You have given Your angels charge over me to keep me in all my ways. Father, today I employ the help of Your angelic host. Father, You said in Your word that You encamp the Angel of the Lord around those who fear You. I declare that as I release Your divine word that You would release the angelic help I need to see the answer to my petitions. I declare that every angel that has been assigned to assist me and minister to me be released with great power to accomplish the assignments given to them on my behalf for this day. Father, I thank You that even as Your word has been released You have opened up Your heavens and released legions of angels to be strategically placed in the areas that I will go to today, in the name of Jesus. I thank You that you have released angels to guard and protect my family, territory, and possessions. I thank you, Lord, that angels excel in strength as I praise and worship You in song; may they break forth with great power against the enemy that has risen up against me, in the name of Jesus.

Father, You said in Your word that one can put a thousand to flight and two can put ten thousand to flight, so Father, I thank You that as I pray the enemy is being scared by the angelic host in seven different ways and they flee from sight of the Captain of the Hosts. I declare that strong and mighty warrior angels do battle and prevail against any strongman and his demonic horde that would try to withstand the angel who comes with the answer to my prayers. I bind the strongman and those who operate with him, and I declare that the purposes, strategies, plans, devices, plots, schemes, ploys, snares, and traps are aborted and come to nothing, in the name of Jesus. I thank You, Lord, that the demonic hosts, as I release Your word, are being smitten with blindness. I declare that they walk in dark and slippery places with the angel of the Lord afflicting them. I declare that they fall into the pit that they have dug for me; let their tongues be divided and let the works of their hands be frustrated and die, in the name of Jesus. Let the Hosts of Heaven attack with the lightning force of the Almighty, swiftly and utterly destroying them, in the name of Jesus. I declare that the rulers of darkness and the wickedness in the high places over my life are now dethroned, overthrown, pulled down, and destroyed, in the name of Jesus. I declare that every weapon created against me not only shall not prosper, but it will be turned against the wicked to bring their destruction and death, in the name of Jesus. Let a phalanx (foot soldiers in a strategic formation for conquest) be released with great strength and power to cause the enemy that tries to come against me to falter, fail, and be destroyed, in the name of Jesus.

Now Father, I thank You for the angelic host that has been assigned to me. I thank You that they surround me with chariots of fire, and I know that there be more with me than there are with them. I thank You, Lord, for Your divine protection over my life, in Jesus name, Amen.

PRAYER OVER PASTORS

Father, I thank You this day that You are my Shepherd that provides for me, causes me to rest near still waters, restores my soul, and causes my cup to run over.

Father, this day I lift up the pastors whom You have placed in my life to equip me that I may grow in spiritual understanding. Father, I thank You that they are a man and woman of God after your own heart. I thank You that they daily seek Your face for direction, instruction, wisdom, knowledge, and vision for our church family. I thank You that my pastors are kingdom minded, that they establish your will on this earth, and that they expand Your word throughout the world as they edify the people whom You have assigned to them. I thank You, Lord, that their ears are attentive to hear what Spirit of God has to say to His people. I thank You that their eyes are upon You and they flow and operate under the anointing of Issachar, that they may know and discern the opportunities You have set up and doors You have opened for them. I thank You that they have been anointed for such a time as this to preach the gospel, open blind spiritual eyes, bring healing to the wounded and broken, and set the captives free, in the name of Jesus. I thank You that they flow under the power of the Holy Spirit, they speak with new tongues, they lay hands on the sick and they recover, they walk in the power and authority given to them to cast out demons and speak to dry bones that they may live, in the name of Jesus. I thank You Lord, that You give them innovative ideas and have given them out of the box thinking that they reach the people with the Gospel of Jesus Christ. I thank You that they have wisdom in winning souls, that when they minister, they minister with great power and authority. I thank You that the words they speak are spoken with clarity, and understanding, and they are words spoken in due season to bring healing and deliverance to Your people, in the name of Jesus. I thank You, Lord, that the pastors and their families have no need or want; they walk in divine health, healing, and favor all the days of their lives. I declare that they increase more and more, in the name of Jesus. I declare that my pastors have been chosen, anointed, and appointed to do a great work, so I call in resources, goods, and financial blessing to come to them from the four corners of the earth. I declare that they are channels of blessings where finances can flow and multiply, in the name of Jesus. I thank You, Lord, that even in their personal lives their marriage is blessed, that their relationship with You is reflected and seen in and through their relationship with You. I thank You that they are of one heart, one mind, united to each other and united with You, in the name of Jesus. Father, give them of your supernatural strength in their spirits, souls, and bodies to continue to do the work to which You have called them. Lord, I thank You that they will walk and not be weary and they will run and not faint. I thank You that everything that they have sown in the lives of Your people may be harvested unto them good measure, pressed down and shaken together, in the name of Jesus. I thank You that they faithfully study to show themselves approved unto You, workmen that need not be ashamed, rightly dividing the word of truth. By the word they lead me and by the word they discipline, correct, reprove, and train in righteousness that we may bring forth fruit for the glory of God.

Father, I take authority over every satanic spirit and agenda that has been formed against the pastors, in the name of Jesus. I bind spirits of greed, stinginess, pride, adultery and sexual immorality, sickness and disease, witchcraft and sorcery, ill spoken words, feelings of unworthiness, defeat, disappointments, guilt and condemnation, lack, poverty, insufficiency, Jezebelic spirits, false teachings, and false doctrine and any other demonic spirit that would try to bring them down, in the name of Jesus. I declare that every strategy of the enemy, every scheme, everything the enemy has planned, is planning, or will plan is to come to nothing, in the name of Jesus. I speak that fire walls, mighty warrior angels, and the blood of Jesus surround them, keep them, and protect them, in the name of Jesus.

Now Father, I thank You for pastors after Your own heart that care for and watch over Your sheep. I thank You, God, that their reward daily comes to them for putting diligent hands to the plow and doing Your labor of love. Father, keep them in Your unconditional love, in Your perfect peace, and in Your joy that is unspeakable and full of glory, in Jesus name. Amen.

PRAYER FOR PROGRESS AND SUCCESS

Father, I thank You that You are the One that leads me and guides me into my divine destiny; You are the one that opens doors for me that no man may shut. You cause me to triumph!

Father, this day I submit myself to Your divine plans for me. Your word says that Your plans for me are plans of good and not of evil to bring me to an expected end. Father, I thank You that You're anointing me to excel and progress and have good success fall mightily on me today, in the name of Jesus. Father, just as Daniel had a spirit of excellence, I thank You that in whatever I do and wherever I go that excellence will flow through me, in the name of Jesus. Lord, I thank You that Your word says that the hand of the diligent it maketh rich; so Father, on this day I declare that my hands will labor before You in diligence that whatever I touch multiplies and becomes fruitful, in the name of Jesus. I thank You that Your favor rests on me as it did with Joseph, that no matter what I do prospers because You are always with me. I thank You for enabling me to move forward, onward, and upward. I declare that Your grace is on me and I have the mind of Christ to see things and do things as He did, in the name of Jesus. I thank You that through You I do great works that glorify my Heavenly Father. Father, I thank You that this day You have already created multitudes of opportunities for me, You have given me creative ideas, and You have already sent answers to difficult challenges and situations. I thank You that innovative thoughts are already flooding my mind for this day and Your Holy Spirit leads me as they are carried out with excellence. I declare that this day You planted me in my Eden and you have caused me to enter into my Promise Land.

Father, I declare today that I have the anointing to overcome disappointments, setbacks, challenges, hindrances, obstacles, negative attitudes and negative thoughts, and every other spirit that would try to frustrate the works of my hands. I declare that the works of Satan's hands be frustrated; let them fail and come to complete destruction. Let every hidden plan, ill spoken word, and agenda be exposed and brought to destruction now, in the name of Jesus. Let everything that would stand in the way of my progress and success be overthrown, pulled down, rooted out, and consumed by fire, in the name of Jesus. Let barriers, all limitations, and boundaries that were set up as a means to enclose and entrap me be destroyed, in the name of Jesus. Let great changes occur today on my behalf and in my favor, in the name of Jesus. Let all goods, resources, and everything that is beneficial that would advance Your agenda for my life that are residing in the wrong hands be taken by force and turned over into my hands, in the name of Jesus.

Now Father, I thank You that every buried vision, dead dream, imprisoned potential, gift, calling, talent, and skill live and be fruitful, in the name of Jesus. I command them to come forth and activate for the advancement of God's Kingdom, in the name of Jesus. I thank You, Father, for expanding my thinking and giving me out of the box ideas. Father, I thank You, for You have blessed me today with the Joseph Anointing to prosper in the works of my hands. Everything, Father, that has been assigned to be transferred into my hands let it be transferred to the overflow, in the name of Jesus. The Issachar Anointing is to know the times and seasons of opportunity that I may hit the mark and act on the divine ideas that you give to me, and I thank You for Joshua's Anointing, that I may be of a good courage and go forth and take dominion of the territories that You have assigned for me. I declare that this is my day of fruitfulness, productivity, increase, breakthrough, multiplication, expansion, progress, and success. I declare that I am the head and not the tail, I am above and not beneath, I am blessed going in and blessed going out. This day I declare that You have brought me into my wealthy place, in Jesus name. Amen.

PRAYER TO CALL FORTH YOUR CHILDREN'S DESTINY

Father, I thank You this day for being my Heavenly Father who created me with a divine design, purpose, and destiny. I thank You that I can come to Your throne of grace and lift up my children before You, speak Your word over them, and declare that their divine destiny come forth, in the name of Jesus.

Father, I put forth my petitions concerning my children's destiny, calling, purpose, and the anointing that they have been born with, in the name of Jesus. Father, this day I thank You that You would give me, first of all, the wisdom, insight, foresight, knowledge, and understanding to minister to my children according to their divine purpose, call, and destiny. Help me to see their gifts and calling; help me to bring them out, nurture them, and develop them that my children may walk in the works that You have predestined for them. Father, I thank You that You have already placed mentors in their lives that would help me to minister to them, that they may grow up firmly planted in Your word, that they may bear fruit for Your glory.

Father, just as Samson's destiny and Jesus' destiny were revealed to their parents, reveal to me and show me my children's destinies. Show me exactly how they are to be taught of You that they may walk on the path that You have set for them. By faith I declare that their destinies are sealed in the blood of Jesus and in the Holy Spirit. I declare that nothing and no one is able to abort the process necessary for them to operate in their God-given destinies, in the name of Jesus. I call forth now their gifts, talents, skills, and anointing to be activated. I declare that they all know You from a tender age, even as Samuel did, in the name of Jesus. I declare that their minds are the mind of Christ and that your wisdom rests in them. Father, I decree my children will not miss their mark, they will not walk in the wilderness of ignorance, they will not be given over to strange doctrines, beliefs, schools of thoughts, vain perspectives, and foolish speculations. They shall not be moved from the faith that is being taught them, but instead they will store the word of God in their hearts. I decree that my children shall reign, rule, and take dominion of the territories that have been assigned to them that the nations that come after them will be nations of kings and priests, in the name of Jesus.

Eagle of my children's destiny take flight now and soar above the storm and come to your expected end, in the name of Jesus.

Father, I take authority and break the demonic powers that would try to abort my children's destinies. I come forcefully and violently against the spirits of rebellion, disobedience, sexual immoralities and impurities, homosexuality, prostitution, gangs, spirit of Belial, drug addictions, violence, anger, depression, suicide, perverse thinking and wicked imaginations, lost concentration and focus, complacency, indifference, lack of motivation, disappointments, demonic limitations, boundaries and barriers, fear, doubt, unbelief, spirits of witchcraft and sorcery, mental illnesses, strongholds of the mind, sickness and diseases, alcoholism, a revelry spirit, and every satanic and malicious spirit, in power of blood and the name of Jesus. Let the angelic host assigned to warfare on my children's behalf be released with great force, might, and power against the principalities, powers, rulers of darkness, and spiritual wickedness that would try to stand against my children and their destinies. Let them fight, defend, and enable the assigned destinies of my children to break forth like the morning sun, in the name of Jesus. Let satanic hordes be utterly destroyed by your spear and javelin; Lord God, let them be overthrown and come to ruin, in the name of Jesus. NO WEAPON FORMED AGAINST MY CHILDREN IS ABLE TO PROSPER! Lord, You are their Shield and their Buckler; You are their Rearguard, so I say again, :NO WEAPON FORMED AGAINST MY CHILDREN IS ABLE TO PROSPER!"

Now Father, I thank You that my children's destinies will be accomplished. They will fulfill and live in your Edenic anointing which is to take dominion, subdue, be fruitful, and multiply. I call them blessed; I call them the Lord's Anointed. LET THEIR DESTINIES COME NOW, in Jesus name. Amen.

PRAYER FOR MOTHERS-TO-BE

Father, I thank You this day that You are my Heavenly Father who blesses me to be fruitful and who has heard my prayers for the blessing of having children.

Father, I thank You that the fruit of my womb is blessed and like Hannah I will set myself in agreement for my child as I give my offering for him/her that he/she may be in Your service and do the things that You have anointed him/her to do. I thank You that my child will know You at a young age, hear Your voice, and like Samuel he/she will say to You, "Lord here I am." Father, I thank You that even as the angel visited Manoah's wife to tell her how to raise Samson, so do I receive Your wisdom, knowledge, instruction, and direction on how to raise my children that they may fulfill their purpose and calling for their lives, in the name of Jesus. Father, I thank You that the child that You have blessed me with will be an arrow in the hand of the skilled archer; he/she will hit the mark of his/her destiny and will not be deterred. I thank You, Lord, that this child that You have given me is anointed and will grow daily in the spirit and in wisdom. Lord, I thank You that as I go through this pregnancy, You would keep me and my child, that everything that travels through my DNA strand, my blood line, and everything else that will shape and form him/her comes directly from You, Spirit, in the name of Jesus. Father, I thank You that even as this child is being born there will be no complications, no unnatural bleeding, no deformities; Father, nothing that is not within Your original divine design will have any access to us, in the name of Jesus. I declare that angels are assigned to my child and me that we may both come through this pregnancy healthy and whole, nothing broken and nothing missing, in the name of Jesus.

Father, I declare that Your Spirit rest over my child, that You hold us both in the palm of Your hands, so Father, in the name of Jesus I declare that the doctors, nurses, midwives, and care givers will be men and women of God who will be sensitive to Your presence and who will minister to us with love, mercy, and compassion, with skill and knowledge to know what to do and how to do, in the name of Jesus. I declare that there will be no miscarriages, no physical or mental disabilities or deformities, no post partum syndrome, in the name of Jesus. Every power and principality that tries to upset this pregnancy or birth I declare to be consumed. Let their plans and purposes be aborted and die, in the name of Jesus.

Father, I thank You for a safe pregnancy and child birth. Thank You that my child is covered in Your blood and as he/she enters into this world, Father, begin to temper his/her spirit, begin to develop this child's mind that he/she may serve You at a young age. I call forth his/her gifts, calling, anointing, and talents and I dedicate them

PRAYER FOR MOTHERS-TO-BE

now to the Lord Jesus Christ that the Lord God may be glorified. My child is blessed, covered, and sealed in the Holy Spirit, in the name of Jesus I pray. Amen.

PRAYER FOR PEACEFUL SLEEP

Father, I thank You, Lord, for being my Sun and Shield and the Lifter of my head throughout this day. I thank You, Father, that You shined Your face with favor on my behalf today and You blessed me with peace that passes all understanding.

Father, I thank You that at the closing of this day You would grant me and my entire household sweet sleep tonight. Father, I declare that all the cares of the day for me and my household are placed at the foot of the cross. Let our minds be at peace and at rest as we lay our heads down to sleep. Lord, You said in Your word that as I lay down and slept, I would awaken again, for the Lord sustains me. I thank You that even while we sleep you sustain us and awaken us well refreshed in our bodies and our minds. Father, I thank You that You would guard our dreams, protect us in our dreams, speak to us in our dreams, and keep us from sinning against You in our dreams. Father, thank You that while we are asleep you set warrior angels strategically around us and our home, in the name of Jesus.

Place firewalls, the anointing, and a bloodline around us and our home that we may be safe from every hurt, harm, and danger seen and unseen. Father, I thank You that You are our rest and we do rest safely in You. I thank You that all the toils of the day are released from us as we lift up our hands in prayer as an evening sacrifice. You take our burdens and replace them with rest. You make us to lie down near Your rivers of water that we may be well rested and refreshed. You are the Restorer of our souls; you rebuild us even in our sleep from everything that may have been broken during the day or worn down that we may be well strengthened for the next day to continue in our labor of love for the Lord. I thank You, Lord, that while we slumber, everything that is needed for the following day You go before us and prepare the way and You go out and make the crooked places straight.

Father, I come against tormenting spirits of the mind, fear, nightmares, sleeplessness and insomnia, worries and anxiety that would rob me of sleep, stress and frustrations that come against me in the day and anything else that would try to rob me and my household of our sleep. In the name of Jesus, let everything that would try to steal our sleep, torment us in our dreams, or bring fear and intimidation be bound and consumed in the fire of God. Let them be driven to torment and frustration and cause them to be rendered ineffective, powerless, and useless, in the name of Jesus. You said in Your word, Father, that we should not be afraid for the terror of night but to safely abide under the shadow of Your wings. No weapon that is formed against me or my household is able to prosper.

Now Father, I thank You that You would bless us with sweet

sleep. I thank You that we will rise early in the morning and sing praise with the song that You place in our hearts. I thank You, Father, that even when we sleep we do so confidently and peacefully, knowing that You are the God that guards and keeps us. You, Lord, never sleep nor slumber but You keep our souls. I thank You once again that You are our rest and peace, in Jesus name. Amen.

PRAYER BEFORE READING GOD'S WORD

Lord God, I come before You this day thanking You for being my Wisdom and the Revealer of hidden truths. You are my light that dispels the darkness of my ignorance concerning Your word.

Father, You said in Your word to study to show myself approved unto You, a workman that needs not be ashamed, rightly dividing the word of truth. You also said that every scripture is God breathed, given by Your inspiration and is profitable for instruction, reproof, and correction of error, discipline in obedience, and for training in righteous, that the man of God may be complete and proficient, well fitted and thoroughly equipped for every good work. Father, I thank You for blessing me with the Holy Spirit who is my teacher and guide into all truth and spiritual understanding and is the one that brings all things back to my memory. I thank You, Lord, that You said that if I lack wisdom to ask it of You who freely gives, so Father, as I get ready to study Your word and plant it in my heart, I ask that You grant me a spirit of wisdom and revelation in the deep and intimate knowledge of You. Let the eyes of my heart be flooded with light, so that I may know and understand the hope to which You have called me and how rich is Your glorious inheritance in the saints. Lord, oh that I may know and understand what is the immeasurable and unlimited and surpassing greatness of Your power in and for us who believe, as demonstrated in the working of Your mighty strength, which You exerted in Christ when You raised Him from the dead and seated Him at Your right hand in the heavenly places. I thank You, Lord, that You would think through me, guide me, and speak to me through Your word those things that You want to reveal to me. Show me, Father, the mysteries that were once hidden, and teach me how to live it that I may reach spiritual maturity, be well equipped, and be firmly planted in Your word and the faith that is now being taught to me. I thank You that what I read will edify, correct, instruct, encourage, and draw me nearer to Your presence. I thank You that as I read everything will become plain, simple, and clearly understood that my spirit man may grow in the knowledge of Christ. I open myself to receive of the Holy Spirit truth and wisdom, in the name of Jesus.

Father, in the name of Jesus, I take authority over mind binding spirits, distractions, cares of my daily living, lost concentration and focus, weariness in my mind and body, and I release a hunger and desire for Your word. I release physical and mental strength to sit under the teaching of the Holy Spirit, for Your words are spirit and life, health and healing to my very bones. I declare and decree because I am meditating on Your word I will not be tossed to and fro with every wind of doctrine but I am firmly rooted on the word.

Father, I thank You that as I read, study, and meditate on Your word I gain skillful, godly wisdom that will make my life pleasing to You. I thank You that as a result I will have the life You predestined for me and I will accomplish Your divine purpose and will for my life. Thank You, Lord, for Your divine wisdom that will be imparted into my life, in Jesus name. Amen.

PRAYER AGAINST SUICIDE

Father, I come before Your presence acknowledging You as the Strength of my life and the One who gives me life and life more abundantly. In You I move and have my being. Lord, you are the air I breath and you are my all in all.

Father, You are the one who keeps and guards my soul. Lord, I am oppressed on every side but by Your grace I am not crushed. I speak life to the situations around me; I speak life to my inner self. I thank You, Lord, that as I cling to Your word that You show me the path of life, in Your presence is fullness of joy, at Your right hand there are pleasures forevermore. Father, I put before You my situation, test, trial, tribulation, circumstances, and I ask that You deliver me, for You have said that You would not see the righteous forsaken. Lord God, give me the strength to endure under the weight of what I am going through. Breathe Your breath of life into me, revive me, and show me Your light in the midst of this darkness. Remove from my mind thoughts of suicide and death, for I know that You are with me even in this time of storm. Rescue me, oh God, out of the hand of the wicked one. Be my Rock and my Refuge, my

Stronghold, and my Fortress. I declare now in the midst of this storm that I will live and not die! I will live and declare the works of the Lord and with long life You have satisfied me; I will live and not die!

Father, You are the one who contends with the enemy that contends with me; take hold of my shield and buckler, and stand up for my help. Draw out Your spear and javelin; close up the way of those who pursue me, and say to me, "I am your deliverance!" Come to my help, oh God, for my help is in the name of the Lord! Rise up on my behalf, oh Lord, of Hosts and let my enemies be scattered. In the name of Jesus, I speak to the demon of suicide that is seeking my life and I say You will not have it, for I am blood bought and redeemed! I bind the spirits of suicide, thoughts of death, oppression, depression, and I call upon the angel of the Lord to pursue, afflict, and cause them to be driven to the pit like the chaff is driven by the wind. I call to be exposed and destroyed completely every plan, scheme, plot, and ploy of the devil against me now, in the name of Jesus. Let every demonic agenda and demonic movement against my life be paralyzed and consumed in the fire of God now, in the name of Jesus. I declare it with the voice of life of God that I will live, I will not die, I have a purpose, I have strength, I can do all things through Christ, I will live! Oh, send out Your light and your truth; let them lead me; let them bring me to Your holy hill and to Your dwelling that I may declare to You, God, You are my exceeding Joy!

Father, I chose to rejoice in the knowledge that You hear my prayers, that I am in the palm of Your hands, that I am on Your mind, and that I am safe in Your presence. I thank You, Lord, that

I dwell in the secret place and under Your wings I do trust. I thank You, Lord, that You saved and took my soul from the hand of my enemy. I rejoice in the knowledge that, Lord, You are good and Your mercy endures forever! I thank You that I am free from the grip of death and I am now in the grip of Your grace. I will live and not die, for Your words to me are spirit and they are life; blessed be the God of my salvation. Thank You, Lord, in Jesus matchless and precious name. Amen.

PRAYER TO OVERCOME FEAR

Father, in the name of Jesus I come before Your presence, thanking You for being my Hiding place, my Strong Tower, and my Refuge.

Father, You said in Your word I should not be afraid of the terror by night, nor of the arrows that flieth by day, nor of the pestilence that walks in darkness, nor of the destruction that wastes at noon day. Father, I trust in You; You are my help and my protection. You said in Your word that You did not give me a spirit of fear but of power, love, and a sound mind. So I declare I shall not be moved by what the enemy brings against me, but I will stand firm knowing that You are my rearguard and a firewall around me. You said in Your word I should not fear, for You hold me up in Your right hand of righteousness and Your perfect love casts out all fear; so everything that would bring fear into my life I call the perfect love of God to cast it out, in the name of Jesus. Father, You said in Your word to fear not but be of good courage, so I thank You that as I face negative circumstances and situations, tests, trials, and tribulation, I will not fear because I am more than a conqueror, I am an overcomer, in the name of Jesus.

Father, I take authority over the spirit of fear, intimidation, anxiety, suspicion, and everything that would rob my joy and peace. I bind it and rebuke it from my life in the name of Jesus. I declare that the spirit of fear and every spirit that is in operation with it is rendered ineffective, powerless, and useless against me, in the name of Jesus. I declare that my mind and heart are free from the affliction and I am delivered from the spirit of fear, in the name of Jesus. I will not be oppressed, I will not walk in darkness, I will not be intimidated because I am of good courage, in the name of Jesus.

Father, I thank You that I am under Your wings, You are my light and my salvation, of whom shall I be afraid? You are my resting place, You are my firm confidence, and I trust in Your word. Lord, I thank You that the spirit of fear is far from me and I walk by faith daily concerning my situations. I thank You, Lord, that in everything I face nothing is too hard or impossible for You and You are the answer to all my situations. I thank You, Lord, for peace of mind, peace in my heart, and freedom to do what You have called me to do, in the name of Jesus. Amen.

PRAYER TO BECOME IMITATORS OF CHRIST

Heavenly Father, I come before Your presence acknowledging You as the Creator God. You created me in Your image and in Your likeness. It is You that made me and not me myself; I am Your sheep and the sheep of Your pasture.

Father, this day I ask that by Your Holy Spirit You help me to be an imitator of Christ and walk in love. Lord, You said in Your word that Your Holy Spirit has made His home in me and that He is my guide and the One that leads me to the Truth. Holy Spirit, I ask that You would help me to walk in uprightness of heart that I may not be corrupted by sin. Help me to love as Christ loved even as His word says that we are to love our enemies that we may show that we are truly children of God. I thank You, Lord, that daily I walk in the fruit of the Spirit so that I may bear good fruit for the heavenly Father. I thank You Lord that You would bless me to have the wisdom of God and that I may have the mind of Christ. I thank You, Lord, that daily You think through me and speak through me that the words that come from my lips would be a fountain of life to the hearer. May what I speak to those around me today bring life and life more abundantly; let it edify them and bring hope to them. I thank You that as I meditate on Your word day and night I will not only be a hearer of Your word but also a doer. I thank You that Your light in me shines before those who surround me that they may see my good works and glorify the heavenly Father which is in heaven. Lord, let my life be a reflection of my relationship with You that You may continually bless me to be fruitful, multiply, and take dominion over the territory You set me over. I thank You, Lord, that daily I can present myself as a living sacrifice and by the Holy Spirit I am able to renew my mind daily that I may not be conformed to this world but be transformed into the image of Christ.

Father, I declare that I do not walk in the flesh but I am led by Your Holy Spirit; therefore, I cancel and make null and void the works of the flesh, the lust of the flesh, the lust of the eyes, and the pride of life. I declare that the old man is stripped away and I am clothed in the new man. I am crucified and the life I live, I live in Christ Jesus. I declare I am clothed in the Lord Jesus Christ, I am a new creature in Christ, the old things are passed, and now new things have come. I declare that I am fearfully and wonderfully created in the image of God. I declare that besetting sins and the things that would try to bind me to the old man are destroyed in the power of the blood of Jesus. I declare that I am free to live a lifestyle of righteousness, holiness, love, joy, and peace in the Holy Spirit.

Father, I thank You that by Your Spirit I am able to walk in a manner pleasing to You. Thank You for perfecting those things

118

concerning me; thank You for enabling me to reflect You to those around me that they may know that You are a God of love, mercy, kindness, and grace. Thank You that this day Your will is being done in my life. May Your light and anointing flow from me to touch others in a special way even as Jesus did, in Jesus name. Amen.

PRAYER TO CAST DOWN WICKED IMAGINATIONS

Father, I come before Your presence, thanking You for being the Great and Mighty one that keeps me in perfect peace.

Father, this day I submit my mind and every part of my mental faculties over to You. I bring You in remembrance of Your word that says if my mind is stayed on You then You would give me perfect peace. Father, today I declare and decree that my mind only thinks on things that are perfect, pure, lovely, and of a good report. Regardless of the situations I face, I make the decision to meditate and rejoice in Your promises for my life. I declare that I think on things that are above. I have the mind of Christ, and the wisdom of God is made in me. I thank You, Lord, that my thoughts are toward You; search me, Father, and remove from me everything that does not bring glory to You in my thought life. Father, I thank You that the meditation of my heart is acceptable to You and You perfect those things that concern me. I thank You, Lord, that I fret not, nor will I be anxious for anything, for You care for me and know my needs even before I bring them to You. I receive Your peace that passes all understanding to rest on the inside of me. Father, I thank You that I need not worry about anything; I lean on you, Lord, and not to my own understanding. In all my ways I will acknowledge You and I thank You for blessing me with the desires of my heart. Father, I thank You that my soul, which is my mind, will, and emotions, is under the control of the Holy Spirit. Father, I thank You that You have made Your ways known to me and I do meditate on Your word day and night. I have hidden Your words in my heart that I may not sin against You, so I surrender my entire soul under Your leadership, Father. Thank You, Lord, for giving me understanding; I will keep Your word and I will observe it with my whole heart. I thank You that my heart and my soul are sound because I cling to Your word.

Father, You said that the weapons of our warfare are not carnal but mighty through God for the pulling down of strongholds, casting down imagination and every high thing that lifts itself against the knowledge of God and bringing into captivity every thought to the obedience of Christ. Father, I take authority over every thought that would try to lift itself against the word of God in me. Every negative thought, every wicked imagination, evil foreboding, worries, fear, fretting, I cast down in the name of Jesus. Father, every mind binding spirit, spirits of confusion, cobwebs of the mind, demonic illusions, twisted perceptions, sexually immoral thoughts, thoughts of murder, suicide, and depression, and every mental affliction, I bind and rebuke in the name of Jesus. I render them ineffective and useless against me, in the name of Jesus. Thoughts of unworthiness, shame, condemnation, all negative thoughts of the devil, I call to be destroyed by the sword of the spirit now, in the name of Jesus. I release now in my mind the peace that passes all understanding, the nine fruits of the Spirit to operate and function in my soul with freedom and gladness, for I am no longer under condemnation for I am in Christ. He is my Burden Bearer, Yoke Destroyer, and Way Maker, so I have no need to fret. I declare that my mind is set firmly on the word of God.

Father, I thank You this day that my mind is free from the bondage of wicked imaginations and negative thoughts. Thank You that daily I renew my mind that I may not be conformed to this world's way of thinking but be transformed unto the image of Christ, in Jesus name I pray. Amen.

PRAYER WHEN MAKING IMPORTANT DECISIONS

Father, I come before Your presence today seeking Your wisdom concerning an important decision that I am to make. Lord, You know my going in and going out, You know my heart and all my ways, so I ask for Your divine wisdom; You are The All Knowing God.

Father, I acknowledge You and I lean not to my own understanding that You may direct my path concerning this decision. Father, Your word says that we should roll our works upon You and Your plans are the ones that will stand. Father, I submit to Your will and Your way even as I make this decision, for Your plans are plans of good and not of evil for me. Father, I ask that You shed truth concerning this decision and allow me to see the things that in my haste I would otherwise miss. Father, give me the patience to wait on You as You lead and direct me in the correct course of action concerning this decision. Lord, You said in Your word that the thoughts of the diligent tend only to plenteousness, but everyone who is impatient and hasty hastens only to want. Lord, allow Your Holy Spirit to lead me and guide me in the decision making process that I may not be led by the desires of my flesh into lack and want. Lord, even as the High Priest consulted You and those men and women of faith who were faced with difficult decisions turned to You, so I now turn to you to lead me in the right direction. I ask for confirmation, Lord, as You said in Your word let everything be established by two or three witnesses; Lord, I will not move until You have confirmed to me that the decision I make is the right one. Father, give me discernment to know what is right from what is wrong and to know truth behind the lie. Father, I receive Your clear instructions and directions concerning this decision now, in the name of Jesus. Lord, send godly people of wisdom that in and through them You may speak to me and reveal to me what my next step should be.

Lord, this day I cast down selfish thoughts, greed, self gain, lustful desires for deceitful riches, demonically influenced thoughts that came from the counsel of the wicked, and I am open to and receive now Your divine counsel, Your skillful and godly wisdom, knowledge, and understanding. Let every demonic utterance that would try to move me from the path that God sets me on die from its root, in the name of Jesus.

Father, thank You. I trust You and confidently await Your instructions and guidance. I thank You that You are already setting things in motion, moving godly trusted people to speak into my life, and You are placing me in the right place at the right time that I may make the right decision. Thank You, Lord, that You are my Shepherd who leads me on the path of righteousness. I rest in You confidently and I will wait upon You as You establish my steps and direct them by Your word. Father, I thank You for going with me through this process and I know that I will have the answer to this petition, in Jesus name. Amen.

PRAYER OF REPENTANCE TO RECEIVE SALVATION

Lord God, I humbly come before Your presence seeking mercy. I know You to be the God who is love, whose mercy endures forever, and You are a God of grace.

Lord God, I come to You according to Your word that if I confess my sins that You are faithful and just to forgive me and cleanse me of all unrighteousness. Lord, I acknowledge and confess my sins to You; I confess that I have broken Your holy law and I am in need of a savior. You said, Lord, that a broken and a contrite spirit You will not turn away. I am broken before You, Lord, because of my sins that are before me. I ask for Your forgiveness. Lord, forgive me of all my sins in thoughts, in words, and in actions. Everything that I have done in the past and present, Lord, I ask that You forgive and release me from the penalty of sin, for the wages of sin is death. Lord, You said in Your word that if I confess with my mouth the Lord Jesus Christ and believe it in my heart I will be saved. Lord, I believe that You came in the flesh, You were born of a virgin, You died on the cross to pay for my sins, and on the third day you rose from the dead. Lord Jesus, cleanse me with Your precious blood of all my sins; forgive me, Lord. I receive You as my Lord and personal Savior. Do not erase, dear Lord, my name from the Lamb's book of Life. I surrender my spirit, soul, and body to your Lordship.

Now in the name of Jesus, let every attachment to the world, every care that entangles me in sin, every besetting sin, the lust of the flesh, the lust of the eyes, and the pride of life be destroyed by the power of the blood of Jesus. Every shackle, bondage, fetter, yoke, and chain of the devil that was on my life, Lord Jesus, destroy it now by Your power and by Your anointing, in the name of Jesus. Every negative thought of shame, guilt, and condemnation regarding my past sins I reject and refuse to come under now, in the name of Jesus. I render those thoughts ineffective, powerless, and useless against me, in the name of Jesus.

Father, I thank You that I am now no longer under condemnation because I am in Christ. I thank You that I am now a new creature in Christ, the old things are passed away, and now the new things have come. I thank You, Lord, that now I am the righteousness of God in Christ Jesus. I am blood bought and redeemed. I thank You, Lord, that as I placed my trust and faith in You that You justified me from the guilt of sin. I thank You for the free gift of eternal life, Lord God, that I received through Jesus Christ. I thank You, Lord, that my mind is now the mind of Christ, that the Holy Spirit is now living on the inside of me. I thank You that the life I live I live it through Christ Jesus. Father, I thank You for Your saving grace; thank You for loving me even when I was dead in my sins. I thank You, Lord Jesus, that you have restored me to right relationship with the Father. I AM FORGIVEN, RECONCILED WITH THE FATHER, AND HAVE BEEN SET FREE! WHOM THE SON SETS FREE IS FREE INDEED! In Jesus name I pray. Amen.

PRAYER FOR GOD'S ANOINTING

Father, I come before Your presence today and I thank You that You are the God of new things, and fresh anointing.

Lord, I thank You that You empower me and equip me for success, and just as the men and women of faith were anointed for success in their calling, so You have anointed me that I may have all the resources to fulfill the assignment that You have given me for today, in the name of Jesus. Father, even as I pray let Your anointing be activated in me so that Your name may be glorified.

Father, I thank You for fresh, uncommon anointing today. Father, I thank You for the Cyrus anointing for financial increase, where the abundance of the sea is converted unto me. Thank You, Lord, for Esther's anointing of kingdom favor and kingdom strategies, in the name of Jesus. Father, I thank You for releasing Moses' anointing over me to become a trail blazer, a leader, and a deliverer of the spiritually oppressed, in the name of Jesus. Father, thank You for Elisha's anointing for servant hood, for succession, and for a double portion of jurisdiction, of power, and of authority. Activate within me Joshua's anointing to conqueror territories and remove the enemy from what rightfully belongs to me. Let Joseph's anointing for prosperity rest on me that everything I touch may prosper because You are with me. I activate the Edenic anointing that according to the word of the Lord I am blessed to multiply and be fruitful, in the name of Jesus. Father, let the Abrahamic blessing rest on me, for I am a partaker as an adopted child of God. Lord, grant me the Isaachar anointing to know the times and seasons when doors are opened and opportunities are lined up for me, in the name of Jesus. I activate the Solomonic anointing for supernatural wisdom, knowledge and understanding, discernment that I may be a capable steward over the goods that are given me. Grant a Davidic anointing that I may warfare against the Goliaths that would stand in my way trying to intimidate me and keep me from my destiny, in the name of Jesus. Above all, I receive the Anointing of the Holy Spirit that breaks every yoke and every bondage off of my life, in the name of Jesus.

Lord, I thank You that this day will be a day of supernatural breakthrough, miracles, favor, blessings, and all the anointing that has been activated has already made a way for me to have good success. Thank You, Lord, for favoring me this day with all of Your anointing, in Jesus name. Amen.

PRAYER AGAINST ANGER

Father, I thank You that You are the God of Peace, You still the raging storms, and You are my bridge over troubled waters.

Father, I come before Your presence seeking help in this time concerning the spirit of anger. Lord, You said in Your word that a person who has anger is like a city without wall. You also said that we are to be angry and sin not, so Father I come to You that You may remove from me anger concerning the situation that I face. Lord, in Your word You said that good sense makes a man restrain his anger and it is his glory to overlook transgression. Help me, Lord, to walk in love concerning this situation; just as You overlook my faults and are quick to forgive, help me to quickly forgive, in the name of Jesus. Lord, help me to be like the wise man that holds back his anger rather than utter it all. Help me not to be a man of wrath who stirs up strife or causes contention, but Lord, help me to be a peacemaker, led and guided by Your Holy Spirit. Lord, wrath is cruel and anger is like an overwhelming flood. Lord, I am angry because _____;

release me from the anger and give me Your peace that passes all understanding. Lord, You said be angry and sin not, so I confess to You the things that are causing me to get angry that You may release me from them and help me see things from Your perspective of love. Holy Spirit, minister to me in Your still, small voice, for a soft answer turns away wrath. Father, I make a decision even now to let this situation go into Your hands and I surrender to You all of my emotions and thoughts concerning it; I instead receive Your wisdom and peace of mind, in the name of Jesus. Father, let my thoughts turn to those things that are perfect, pure, lovely, and of good report; my mind is now stayed on You that I may receive Your divine wisdom.

Father, right now in the name of Jesus I bind the demon spirits of anger, wrath, rage, violence, vengeance, bitterness, unforgiveness, malice, and spiteful thinking. I cast them to the pit of hell and forcefully cast off the fetter that would try to bind me and cause me to speak, think, and do things under the spirit of anger, by the power of the blood and the name of Jesus. Lord, I release Your peace, I release Your love and Your forgiveness, and I command my soul and flesh to walk in the fruit of the Spirit of self control. I will not give in to the demonic, but I now surrender to the Holy Spirit of God.

Father, I thank You that You release me from anger; I am free from bitterness and unforgiveness. I thank You, Lord, that anger does not have a hold on me because I submit myself to You that the devil may flee from me. Father, I thank You for giving me wisdom on how to control anger; thank You for helping me to

trust You in dealing with this situation, and thank You for blessing me with Your peace that passes all understanding as it rests and rules in my heart, in Jesus name. Amen.

PRAYER AGAINST THE VAGABOND SPIRIT

Father, in the name of Jesus I come before Your throne of grace acknowledging You as the awesome and mighty God of my life. You are the Shepherd that leads me in the paths of my life with Your staff to guide me and Your rod to protect me; You do comfort and restore my soul.

Father, this day I reject the spirit of a vagabond, a wandering spirit. Lord, You said in Your word that You knew me from before the foundation of the world. You created me in Your image and likeness with a purpose and destiny. You said that Your plans for me are plans of good and not of evil, that You hold me in the palm of Your hand, and I am on Your mind. Lord, I thank You that by faith through Christ I am no longer an alien or a stranger; I am not an orphan, but by the Holy Spirit I can testify that You are my Abba Father. Your word, the blood of Jesus, and the Holy Spirit seal me as Your own until the day of redemption. Father, I thank You that I have been adopted into Your household; You said in Your word that if I belong to Christ (and I do) then I am Abraham's offspring and heir according to the promise. I understand that in Christ Jesus I am a son of God through faith. God, I thank You that I AM NOT A SLAVE; I AM A SON OF GOD! I AM NOT AN ORPHAN; I AM A SON OF GOD! I AM BORN OF GOD! I AM NO LONGER AN OUTSIDER; I AM A CITIZEN OF THE KINGDOM OF GOD AND I BELONG TO GOD'S HOUSEHOLD! Lord, I thank You that Your word said what is born of the Spirit is spirit; I walk by the Spirit and I live by the Spirit. I am Your workmanship created in Christ Jesus.

Father, I cast down, rebuke, reject, and make of no effect every wicked, demonic, and satanic thought and feeling of abandonment, rejection, loneliness, the vagabond and wandering spirit of Cain that would have me roaming around in the spirit realm as though I have nowhere to go and have no purpose and destiny. Spirit of a vagabond and of wandering, I rebuke you and release you to wander in the dry places of hell, in the name of Jesus. I declare this day that my identity is sealed, my purpose is sealed, my destiny shall be fulfilled, and I will accomplish the assignments, missions, and above all the will of God for my life. I declare and decree that all the promises of Abraham are now my realities. I am loved, I am on God's mind, and His presence is ever with me. God's word is a lamp to my feet and a light to my path; God guides me on the path of righteousness; therefore, I cancel the lie of the devil that I have no purpose. I cancel the lie that I was born for misery, struggle, mediocrity, low living, having no vision or dreams; I reject it and I declare that I AM BORN OF GOD AND WHATEVER IS BORN OF GOD OVERCOMES, IS FRUITFUL, MULTIPLIES, AND

HAS DOMINION, IN THE NAME OF JESUS!

Father, I thank You that I am Yours and You are mine. I am a chosen generation, a royal priesthood, and a peculiar people. I am the Lord's anointed, I am blessed, I have purpose, I have a mission, I have a destiny, and I belong to God. I am no longer an outsider in darkness, but I am His child translated into the kingdom of His beloved Son. Thank You, God, for being my Heavenly Father, in Jesus name I pray. Amen.

PRAYER FOR FREEDOM FROM SEXUAL IMMORALITY

Father I come before your presence humbly yet boldly to your throne of Grace. I acknowledge you as a Holy God, the God who is a Consuming Fire, you are an Awesome God.

Father, I come to You seeking Your help regarding sexual immorality and impurity. Lord, You said in Your word that he who loves purity will have the king for his friend. I come to You surrendering my body, my mind, and all that I am to You that You would purify me even as with hyssop from this stronghold of sexual vice. Lord, You said that my body is the temple of the Holy Spirit and it is not intended for sexual immorality but it is to honor You, Lord. Forgive me, Father, of the sin of indulging in sexual immorality, indecencies, and impurities. Deliver me, my God, from these strongholds and tendencies that bind me and cause me to return to its filth like a dog to vomit. I lift my hands surrendering all to You; consume by fire the altars that I erected in the high places of my heart that were dedicated to sexual immorality, indecency, and impurity. Come Holy Spirit with fire, with power, and Your glory and cleanse me, purify me, break me, mold me, restore me, renew me in righteousness and holiness. Lord, I forgive those who in my past by some immoral sexual action against me opened demonic doors to my life.

Father, by the power of the blood of Jesus, the yoke destroying, bondage breaking anointing of the Holy Spirit, destroy from my mind, my body, my spirit, my entire being demonic soul ties, the spirit of fornication, adultery, prostitution, pornography, homosexuality and lesbianism, lust and inherited lust, sexual vices, indecent and impure sexual images and thoughts, altar of the heart dedicated to sexual demons, unholy desires, sexual addictions, seducing spirits, sexual strongholds, bondages, chains, fetters, proclivities, besetting sins. Father, consume them all to ashes and let Your power abolish, eradicate, pull down, overthrow, and annihilate doors of the past that were open to these demonic principalities through rape, incest, molestation, sexual contact done in ignorance or knowingly in my childhood, in the name of Jesus. I cancel now every other spirit that was released in my life as a result of sexual immorality, indecency, and impurities. Spirits of shame, guilt, condemnation, fear, low self worth and self esteem, deception and lies, anger, suicide, violence, I command be consumed and utterly destroyed from my life, in the name of Jesus. SPIRIT OF SEXUAL LUST LOOSE ME, RELEASE ME, AND LET ME GO NOW BY THE POWER OF THE BLOOD OF JESUS!

Father, I thank You that this is a new day; I receive your

forgiveness, I receive healing for my soul and spirit, I receive freedom from these demonic entities and let every demonic door that was open now be closed, shut, and locked, in the name of Jesus. Father, I thank You for Your mercy and Your grace as You showed it to the woman who was caught in adultery. Thank You, Lord, for restoring me and I ask from this day onward that You help me by Your Holy Spirit to live upright before You, in all righteousness and pureness of heart, in Jesus name I pray. Amen.

PRAYER FOR RECEIVING MIRACLES

Father, I come before Your presence and I acknowledge You as the God of wonders, Creator of Heaven and Earth whose power no enemy can withstand.

Father, this day I acknowledge You as the Miracle working God. God, I thank You that the areas in my life that seem impossible to me, Lord, by Your miracle working power will be released and bring about the supernatural change that I am believing You for, in name of Jesus. Lord, even as the children of Israel saw Your marvelous power at work on their behalf, so now, Father, stretch Your hand against the enemy that seeks to keep my life imprisoned and without hope; swallow the enemy up in that spiritual Red Sea, in the name of Jesus. Lord, I thank You that even as Joshua cried out in the midst of battle and You responded by causing the walls of Jericho to fall and even the solar system to stand still, so now, Lord, break forth into my natural situation that I face with Your supernatural might, in the name of Jesus. Father, You are no respecter of persons and

PRAYER FOR RECEIVING MIRACLES

You said to remember the former things and to put You in remembrance of Your word, so Lord now let me declare Your mighty works. You are the God that caused David to defeat Goliath in his youth; You gave power to Elijah to call fire from heaven, to shut up the heavens preventing rain; You gave power to Elisha to cause the ax head to float on water, to open the eyes of his servant to see the angelic host, to resurrect a little boy, and even in death to resurrect a fallen soldier when he touched the bones of Elisha. You multiplied fish and bread in the hands of Jesus. He walked on water, calmed the storms, healed the sick, resurrected the dead, and so did His disciples. So now I declare let the miracle working power of Christ be released in my life over the situations that seem impossible. I declare now that You are the same yesterday, today, and forever more, so Lord God Almighty display Your wondrous working power that all may know that there is a God and His name is Jehovah. Release Your miraculous power over my marriage/relationship, my children, my finances, and my body, in the name of Jesus. Father, let the heavens be opened above me and cause me to walk in the miraculous. Those things that were raised against me that tried to deter me from what is rightly mine, Father, remove it by Your miraculous power, in the name of Jesus.

Now Father, even as You brought plagues on those who withstood Your servants, release Your ten plagues against my enemies that would try to withstand me. Even as Jannes and Jambres, Pharaoh's magicians, greatly feared at your power and declared, "This is not but the finger of God!" so let them quake and tremble. Let them run in confusion, in fear and turmoil and let them kill themselves, in the name of Jesus. Father, just as the angels blinded the men of Sodom, Lord, hit them with blindness and let them walk in darkness, in the name of Jesus. Father, I receive Your miracle working power that turns the impossible to possible, the incredible to credible, the power that causes the mountains to be removed, in the name of Jesus. LORD, I RECEIVE MY MIRACLE TODAY! THE MIRACLE THAT IS DUE ME I HAVE IT NOW, IN THE NAME OF JESUS! FINANCIAL MIRACLES COME TO ME NOW! HEALING MIRACLE COME TO ME NOW! MIRACLE FOR THE RESTORATION OF OUR FAMILY, COME TO ME NOW! I RECEIVE MY MIRACLE, IN JESUS NAME. AMEN!

SOAKING PRAYER WHEN IN WORSHIP

Father, I come before Your presence thanking You, for You are my Joy River and the Lover of my soul. Thank You, Lord, for You are sweeter to me than the honey in a honeycomb.

Lord God, today I desire to be in Your presence. I desire to bask in the beauty of Your holiness. Lord, as You lead me beside the still waters, I thank You for refreshing my soul. I thank You, Lord, that You are my fountain of living waters that restores and renews me each and every day. Lord, in Your presence there is fullness of joy and pleasures evermore, and as Your word says, I would rather stand at the gates of the house of the Lord than enjoy the wicked pleasures of this world. Better is one day in Your courts than a thousand elsewhere. You fill me and satisfy my soul, and with your mercy that endures forever, my God and my King, I thirst for You even as a deer pants and longs for the water in brooks. I ask, Father, that You fill my cup until it overflows in Your love, in Your peace, and in Your joy. As I lift up my hands to You, Lord, in my spirit I pour out my love to You; let my worship be as sweet smelling perfume to You. Father, I thank You for the privilege of being a lover of Your presence. I thank You, Lord, for allowing me to kiss Your face with my words. I receive a fresh anointing, a fresh wind, and a fresh fire as I continually serve You. Let my love for You attract Your presence more and more, for You are the air that I breathe. I can do nothing without You, but with You I can soar on wings of an eagle to my destiny. You cover me under Your wings and I delight myself in them. Lord, how beautiful are your tabernacles; as the train of your glory fills this place, I say with the angels, "HOLY, HOLY IS THE LORD AND THE EARTH IS FULL OF YOUR GLORY!" Let my love for You only increase and never lag in zeal; let my prayers be set before You as the evening sacrifice as I present myself as a living sacrifice. I love You, Lord, more than life; I love you, Lord, because You loved me and chose me from before the foundations of the world. Your love is amazing, the way You loved me even in my sins and You took me out and made me new. You ministered to me reconciliation; You bound me with Your cords of Love, and You uphold me in Your right hand of righteousness. Oh Lord, how wonderful, how awesome, how beautiful is Your presence; surround me and fill me with Your presence. Here I am Lord, at the well of Your presence to drink deeply of You, so that I may thirst no more. You sustain me, You uphold me, You rescue me, You make all things in my life new, and I thank You. Your glory is everlasting; bathe me in the splendor of your light and search my heart, my inner self in the light of Your glory. You give a clean heart, Oh God, and You   blot out all of my transgression. How great is Your love for me and how amazing is Your grace.

Father, I thank You, You are my Song, my Life, and my Love. You refresh me with Your presence and strengthen me with Your Spirit; therefore, I say, "YOU ARE AN AMAZING GOD! I LOVE YOU MORE THAN LIFE!" AMEN.

PRAYER OF RESURRECTION

Father, I come before Your presence acknowledging You as the God that makes all things new. You are the God who gives life and life more abundantly.

Father, this day I put before You my dreams, goals, visions, assignments, ideas, possibilities, and everything that was attached to my destiny that has died and become a valley of dry bones. Lord, those things that were predestined to be activated in my life that would have catapulted me into the next level and dimension of my life and calling that are now in that valley of dry bones I put them before You. Father, those things that would have brought transforming change to my finances, my health, my family, my job situation that are now in the tomb I put before You. Lord, there is nothing too hard or impossible for You. You are the same today, yesterday, and forever; more and You are the Giver of Life.

Father, even as You told the prophet Ezekiel to speak to the dry bones and they lived, with the same power of resurrection with which You raised Christ from the dead, Lord I thank You that same resurrection voice and power are on the inside of me. Lord, I speak

to the valley of dry bones that is before me and I declare O DRY
BONES, HEAR THE WORD OF THE LORD. LET BREATH
AND SPIRIT ENTER YOU, AND I CALL YOU TO LIVE, IN
THE NAME OF JESUS. Let my voice, God Almighty, come forth
like thundering noise and let there be a shaking, a trembling, and let
bone come to bone, sinew come to sinew, and rise up like a mighty
army, in the name of Jesus. I call breath and the Spirit of life to come
from the four winds of the Earth and breathe on this valley. I declare
STAND UP AND LIVE, IN THE NAME OF JESUS. Everything
that is now in the tomb, even as You, Lord Jesus, called Lazarus out,
I declare now to those things COME OUT! DEATH, LOOSE IT,
RELEASE IT, AND LET IT GO, IN THE NAME OF JESUS!
Father, I speak life and life abundantly, in the name of Jesus. I
declare anything that is buried, anything that looks like it's critical
and about to die, Father, I speak with the voice of resurrection and
say LIVE! GET UP! in the name of Jesus. Father, every situation
where it looked like I was defeated, disappointed, set back, Lord, I
declare now BE THOU RESURRECTED AND LIVE, IN THE
NAME OF JESUS! Blow upon the valley, blow upon the tomb, like
a mighty tempest wind. Let Your river of life flood every area with
refreshing, renewal, and revival, in the name of Jesus.

Father, I thank You that all the things that the enemy meant and
plotted for death now live, in the name of Jesus. Everything that the
enemy stole and buried is now returned seven fold, in the name of
Jesus. Lord, the things that were dry are now places of overflow,
abundance, and good, in the name of Jesus. Father, I thank You for
Your resurrection power, in Jesus name I pray. Amen.

HOW PRAYER DECLARATIONS WORK

Remember that what you say today is creating your tomorrow.

It is imperative to understand that your present declarations are becoming your future manifestations.

An important thing to remember when putting these decrees into practical application is to use the word of God as your basis. So when you declare a thing over your life, you speak it in the now with applicable biblical context to back what you are saying. The next step is to identify your problem, find the proper scripture to apply to that situation, and speak the opposite of what you are going through. You may be dealing with sickness or disease today. The worst thing you can do is complain about what you are going through. When you find yourself complaining about something--stop and ask yourself, "What do I want?" If you're sick, talking about how bad you feel or what the doctor said is not the path to shifting from sickness to health. Here is a great example:

HOW PRAYER DECLARATIONS WORK

Father in the name of Jesus, I decree and declare that I am now healed according to your word. I confess according to Isaiah 53:5 that by your stripes I am already healed. I declare that according to 3 John 2, above all things I prosper, I am in health, even as my soul prospers. I thank you that I now walk in divine health.

DAILY POWER DECLARATIONS

I AM NOT GOING BACK BUT I AM MOVING FORWARD IN JESUS NAME!

GOD HAS CHOSEN ME AND I AM WELL ABLE TO DO ANY TASK HE ASSIGNS TO ME!

I DECLARE THAT THERE ARE INCREDIBLE BLESSINGS OVER MY LIFE TODAY!

I DECLARE THAT THERE IS AN EXPLOSION OF GOD'S BLESSINGS OVER MY LIFE!

I DECLARE THAT GOD'S FAVOR IS OVER MY LIFE!

I DECLARE THAT THERE IS SUDDEN INCREASE OVER MY LIFE!

I DECLARE THAT THE ANOINTING OF THE HOLY SPIRIT RESTS, RULES AND ABIDES IN ME IN THE NAME OF JESUS!

DAILY POWER DECLARATIONS

I DECLARE THAT GOD WOULD ENLARGE MY COAST AND KEEP ME FROM EVIL IN THE NAME OF JESUS!

I BELIEVE AND RECEIVE THAT THE STRONGMAN IS BOUND OVER MY LIFE AND EVERY NEGATIVE THING HAS BEEN RETURNED TO THE PIT OF HELL FROM WHENCE IT CAME.

EVERY GENERATIONAL CURSE, WITCHCRAFT, HEX, FREE MASONARY, ANYTHING THAT IS NOT OF YOU GOD I SEND IT BACK TO THE PIT OF HELL FROM WHENCE IT CAME AND I DECLARE MYSELF FREE AND WHOLE IN THE NAME OF JESUS.

I RELEASE THE POWER OF THE HOLY SPIRIT OVER MY LIFE TO GUARD ME AND PROTECT ME IN THE NAME OF JESUS.

I REBUKE EVERY UNCLEAN SPIRIT FROM ITS INFLUENCE OVER MY LIFE IN THE NAME OF JESUS.

I DECLARE THAT GOD IS IN ME THEREFORE WHO CAN BE AGAINST ME? I SHALL NOT FEAR, GOD IS ON MY SIDE.

I DECLARE THAT EVERY PRINCIPALITY RANGED AGAINST ME FALLS INTO THE PIT OF DESTRUCTION IN THE NAME OF JESUS.

I DECLARE THAT I AM COVERED IN THE POWER OF THE BLOOD OF JESUS.

I AM MORE THAN A CONQUEROR, MY BEST DAYS ARE AHEAD OF ME, I AM DESTINED TO WIN.

I AM BLESSED AND HIGHLY FAVORED, GOD HAS A PLAN AND A PURPOSE FOR MY LIFE.

I AM ANOINTED TO PROSPER, I AM HEALED AND WHOLE. THERE IS NOTHING BROKEN AND THERE IS NOTHING MISSING.

I AM AN OVERCOMER, I HAVE NO FEARS, ALL THINGS ARE POSSIBLE TO ME BECAUSE I BELIEVE IN GOD.

I AM THE RIGHTEOUSNESS OF GOD IN CHRIST JESUS, I WALK UNDER OPEN HEAVENS.

I AM DAILY LOADED WITH BENEFITS, THE PEACE OF GOD RESTS ON ME AND HE PERFECTS EVERYTHING CONCERNING ME.

I WALK IN SUCCESS AND PROGRESS, I AM DILIGENT AND IN MY HAND IS THE POWER TO CREATE WEALTH. IN JESUS NAME AMEN!

I SPEAK INCREASE TO COME FROM THE EAST, THE WEST, THE NORTH AND FROM THE SOUTH OVER MY LIFE.

I DECLARE, I WALK BY FAITH AND NOT BY SIGHT TODAY IN THE NAME OF JESUS.

I DECLARE THAT MY TRUST IS IN JESUS CHRIST.

I DECLARE THAT THE WILL OF GOD BE DONE IN MY LIFE.

I DECLARE THAT FEAR, DOUBT, UNBELIEF HAS NO CONTROL AND NO POWER OVER ME IN JESUS NAME.

I DECLARE THAT MY HANDS ARE ANOINTED FOR WEALTH IN JESUS NAME.

I WILL LIVE OUT ALL THE DAYS OF MY LIFE.

I DECLARE THAT THERE IS GREATNESS OVER ME AND I AM HEALED FROM THE CROWN OF MY HEAD TO THE SOLE OF MY FEET.

I DECLARE THAT I WALK UNDER THE WISDOM AND THE ANOINTING OF GOD.

I DECLARE THAT I HAVE THE TONGUE OF THE LEARNED AND WHAT I SPEAK WILL COME TO PASS IN THE NAME OF JESUS.

I DECLARE THAT NO WEAPON THAT IS FORMED AGAINST ME WILL PROSPER. THIS IS MY TIME AND THIS IS MY SEASON IN THE NAME OF JESUS.

I AM A KINGDOM CITIZEN WITH AUTHORITY.

I DECLARE THAT I WILL EXPERIENCE GOD'S FAITHFULNESS TODAY.

I DECLARE I WILL NOT WORRY IN THE NAME OF JESUS.

I DECLARE I WILL PUT MY TRUST IN GOD AND NO OTHER.

TODAY I GIVE BIRTH TO GOD'S PROMISES AND I DECLARE EVERYTHING THAT GOD HAS PROMISED ME I WILL RECEIVE IT.

I WILL WALK IN GOD'S POWER, GOD'S STRENGTH AND GOD'S DETERMINATION.

I AM A KINGDOM CITIZEN.

I AM IN THIS WORLD BUT I AM NOT OF THIS WORLD.

I AM THE RIGHTEOUSNESS OF GOD IN CHRIST JESUS.

I DECLARE I HAVE THE GRACE THAT I NEED FOR TODAY.

I WILL OVERCOME OBSTACLES TODAY, I WILL OUT LAST

CHALLENGES TODAY. I WILL COME THROUGH EVERY DIFFICULT SITUATION THAT THE ENEMY BRINGS MY WAY TODAY IN THE NAME OF JESUS.

I DECLARE THAT IT'S NOT TOO LATE TO ACCOMPLISH EVERYTHING THAT GOD HAS PLACED IN MY HEART.

I DECLARE THAT GOD'S FAVOR FOLLOWS ME EVERYWHERE THAT I GO.

I AM MORE THAN A CONQUEROR.

I HAVE BEEN BORN WITH THE FAVOR OF GOD.

I WILL ACCOMPLISH MY DIVINE DESTINY AND PURPOSE

I DECLARE WHAT I SPEAK OVER MY LIFE WILL COME TO PASS IN THE NAME OF JESUS.

I DECLARE THAT DARKNESS HAS NO POWER OVER ME IN THE NAME OF JESUS.

I DECLARE THAT THE GRACE OF GOD FOLLOWS AND EMPOWERS ME IN THE NAME OF JESUS.

I AM AN AMBASSODOR OF THE KINGDOM.

HOLY SPIRIT PRESERVE ME FROM SIN.

GOD HAS PLEASURE IN THE PROSPERITY OF HIS SERVANTS.

I AM TOTALLY HEALED FROM THE CROWN OF MY HEAD TO THE SOLE OF MY FEET.

I AM THE RIGHTEOUSNESS OF GOD IN CHRIST JESUS.

I AM GIFTED AND ANOINTED TO PREACH THE GOSPEL OF JESUS CHRIST.

MY LIFE IS A LIFE OF HONOR UNTO GOD.

I DECLARE THAT I AM STRONG IN THE LORD AND IN THE POWER OF HIS MIGHT.

I DECLARE THAT I AM NOT A VICTIM OF ANY CIRCUMSTANCE.

I DECLARE THAT I TRUST GOD IN EVERY SITUATION.

I DECLARE THAT I AM LED BY THE SPIRIT OF GOD.

I DECLARE THAT I WALK IN POWER OF GOD'S LOVE

I DECLARE THAT I WILL SEE GOD'S GOODNESS IN MY LIFE TODAY.

I DECLARE THAT MY MIND IS BLESSED AND MY

DAILY POWER DECLARATIONS

THOUGHTS ARE TOWARD CHRIST JESUS.

I HAVE A FRESH ANOINTING ON EVERY SIDE TODAY.

I DECLARE THAT THE ENEMY'S STRONGHOLD HAS NO POWER OVER ME.

MY LIFE IS TRANSFORMED AND MY LIFE IS A LIFE OF HONOR.

THE KINGDOM OF DARKNESS WILL NEVER HAVE POWER OVER MY LIFE.

I DECLARE AND DECREE THAT THERE IS A CONTINUAL ENLIGHTENMENT AND INCREASE OF GOD'S WORD IN MY LIFE.

I DECALRE AND DECREE THAT GOD'S POWER IS RELEASED OVER MY LIFE.

I DECLARE AND DECREE THAT THIS IS DAY OF BREAKTHROUGH, FAVOR, BLESSINGS AND PEACE.

YOU SPIRIT OF WITCHCRAFT, YOUR INFLUENCE AND POWER IS BROKEN OVER MY LIFE IN THE NAME OF JESUS.

THE BLOOD OF JESUS COVERS ME FROM THE CROWN OF MY HEAD TO THE SOLES OF MY FEET.

ANY STRONGHOLD THAT IS OVER MY LIFE IS BROKEN TODAY IN THE NAME OF JESUS.

EVERY FALSE BURDEN THAT HAS BEEN PLACED OVER MY LIFE, I RELEASE IT AND LET IT GO TO THE FOOT OF THE CROSS.

EVERY YOKE OF BONDAGE I DECLARE IT TO BE DESTROYED BY THE POWER OF THE ANOINTING OF THE HOLY SPIRIT.

I DECLARE THAT TODAY I AM IN MY PROMISE LAND, TODAY EVERY BLESSING THAT BEEN ASSIGNED FOR ME TO PROSPER ME COMES TO ME IN THE NAME OF JESUS.

I DECLARE THAT TODAY THE SPIRIT OF GOD WILL GO BEFORE ME AND ESTABLISH PLACES OF FAVOR ON MY BEHALF IN THE NAME OF JESUS.

WICKEDNESS, HEAVY BURDENS AND OPPRESSIONS ARE BROKEN OFF OF MY LIFE NOW AND FOREVER IN THE NAME OF JESUS.

I AM THE RIGHTEOUSNESS OF GOD IN CHRIST JESUS, I AM BORN TO WIN AND DESTINED FOR GREATNESS, AND ON THE INSIDE OF ME GOD'S FAVOR ABOUNDS TO THE OVER FLOW IN THE NAME OF JESUS.

I CLAIM THE PROMISES OF GOD IN MY LIFE AND I RECEIVE THEM BY FAITH IN JESUS NAME.

I DECLARE THAT MY CHILDREN'S DESTINY IS ALREADY OPERATING AND FUNCTIONING IN THEIR LIVES IN THE NAME OF JESUS.

I DECLARE THAT MY POSSESIONS, PROPERTIES, RESOURCES, GOODS AND OPPORTUNITIES BE RELEASED INTO MY HANDS TODAY IN THE NAME OF JESUS.

I DECLARE THAT EVERYTHING THAT PERTAIN TO MY LIFE, FAMILY, CALLING AND MINISTRY BE RELEASED IN A DOUBLE PORTION IN THE NAME OF JESUS.

I DECLARE THAT THIS IS MY DAY OF PEACE, JOY, FAVOR AND INCREASE IN JESUS NAME.

I DECLARE AND I DECREE THE LORD IS MY DEFENSE, I WILL PUT MY TRUST IN HIM, HE WILL DEFEND ME AND FIGHT MY BATTLES FOR ME.

I DECLARE AND DECREE I AM ATTENTIVE TO GOD'S COMMANDMENTS. I PUT MY TRUST IN HIM.

I DECLARE AND I DECREE RESTORATION OF EVERYTHING I LOST IN BATTLE IN JESUS NAME.

I DECLARE AND DECREE THAT EVERYTHING THAT THE ENEMY HAS STOLEN MUST BE RETURNED SEVENFOLD IN THE NAME OF JESUS.

I DECLARE AND DECREE THAT THE THINGS THAT HAVE BEEN WITHELD, HOLD UP AND STOPPED MUST NOW BE RELEASED NOW INTO MY HANDS IN THE NAME OF JESUS.

I DECLARE AND DECREE THAT EVERY GOOD AND PERFECT THING THAT COMES FROM GOD BECOMES MINE IN THE NAME OF JESUS.

I DECLARE AND DECREE THAT I HAVE ACCESS TO THE HEAVENLIES AND SO EVERY SPIRITUAL GIFT NOW BECOMES MINE IN THE NAME OF JESUS.

I AM PLANTED BY THE RIVERS OF WATER AND MY LIFE BRINGS FORTH FRUIT IN THE NAME OF JESUS.

I DECLARE THAT I BRING FORTH FRUIT IN DUE SEASON IN THE NAME OF JESUS.

I DECLARE THAT I AM WISE AND I FOLLOW THE INSTRUCTIONS OF THE LORD.

I DO NOT SIT UNDER THE COUNSEL OF THE UNGODLY BUT MY DELIGHT IS IN THE WORD OF GOD.

YOUR WORD IS A LAMP UNTO MY FEET AND A LIGHT UNTO MY PATH.

I DECLARE THAT I SERVE THE LORD WITH THE FEAR OF THE LORD AND REJOICING.

I DECLARE THAT MY FAITH CAN HANDLE ANYTHING AND THERE IS NOTHING THAT MOVES ME BECAUSE I WALK BY FAITH AND NOT BY SIGHT.

IN THE NAME OF JESUS, LORD YOU ARE MY KEEPER.

I DECLARE AND DECREE THAT YOU SHALL PRESERVE ME AND KEEP ME FROM EVIL IN THE NAME OF JESUS.

I DECLARE AND DECREE THAT YOU WILL PRESERVE MY GOING IN AND GOING OUT.

I DECLARE AND DECREE THAT YOU UPHOLD ME IN YOUR RIGHT HAND OF RIGHTEOUSNESS.

I DECLARE AND DECREE THAT YOU ARE MY LIGHT AND MY SALVATION OF WHOM SHALL I BE AFRAID OF?

I DECLARE AND DECREE THAT YOU SHELTER ME IN THE MIDST OF MY STORMS AND I COME OUT VICTORIOUS IN THE NAME OF JESUS.

I DECLARE AND DECREE THAT YOU ARE MY STRONG

TOWER AND I AM HIDDEN IN YOU FROM THE EVIL THAT MAY COME AGAINST ME IN THE NAME OF JESUS.

I DECLARE AND DECREE THAT I REST IN THE LORD AND WAIT PATIENTLY ON HIM.

I DECLARE AND DECREE THAT THE LORD ORDERS MY STEPS TODAY IN THE NAME OF JESUS.

I BIND THE SPIRIT OF ANGER OVER MY LIFE AND RELEASE THE SPIRIT OF FORGIVENESS IN THE NAME OF JESUS.

I RECEIVE THE SPIRIT OF MEEKNESS AND CAST DOWN THE SPIRIT OF PRIDE IN THE NAME OF JESUS.

I DECLARE AND DECREE THAT FOR A SPIRIT OF HEAVINESS I RECEIVE A SPIRIT OF GLADNESS.

I DECLARE AND DECREE THAT THE LORD GOD PERFECTS THOSE THINGS THAT CONCERNS ME IN THE NAME OF JESUS.

I DECLARE AND DECREE THAT THE MEDITATION OF MY HEART IS ACCEPTABLE TO LORD FOR I MEDITATE ON HIS WORD DAY AND NIGHT IN THE NAME OF JESUS.

I DECLARE AND DECREE THAT THE ADVERSARY IS

UNDER MY FEET.

I DECLARE AND DECREE THAT TRAGEDY IS UNDER MY FEET AND I WALK IN DIVINE PEACE.

I DECLARE AND DECREE THAT MY MIND IS STAYED ON YOU AND I CAST DOWN EVERY WICKED IMAGINATION IN THE NAME OF JESUS.

I DECLARE AND DECREE THAT THE WILL OF GOD FOR MY LIFE IS BEING FULFILLED NOW IN THE NAME OF JESUS.

I DECLARE AND DECREE THAT I WILL NOT FEAR FOR THE UNKNOWN FOR THE PLANS OF GOD TOWARD ME ARE OF GOOD AND NOT OF EVIL.

I DECLARE AND DECREE THAT MY WORD ARE IN AGREEMENT WITH GOD'S DIVINE PURPOSE FOR MY LIFE AND I MOVE FORWARD IN JESUS NAME.

I DECLARE AND DECREE THAT MY YOUTH IS RENEWED LIKE THE EAGLE AND I HAVE STRENGTH TO GO FROM GLORY TO GLORY IN THE NAME OF JESUS.

I DECLARE AND DECREE THAT I OVERCOME EVILWITH GOOD BECAUSE THE HOLY SPIRIT IS IN ME.

I DECLARE AND DECREE THAT THE HOLY SPIRIT

TEACHES ME TO BE HONEST WHEN NO ONE IS AROUND.

I DECLARE AND DECREE THAT I WILL WALK IN PEACE ALL DAY TODAY IN THE NAME OF JESUS.

I DECLARE AND DECREE THAT I AM NOT SLOTHFUL IN THE MY BUSINESS BUT I AM FERVRENT IN MY SPIRIT SERVING THE LORD IN THE NAME OF JESUS.

I DECLARE AND DECREE THAT GOD BLESSES THE WORKS OF MY HANDS TO BE FRUITFUL AND MULTIPLY.

I DECLARE AND DECREE THAT GOD DAILY LOADS ME WITH BENEFITS AND HE CAUSE ME TO DWELL IN MY WEALTHY PLACE.

I DECLARE AND DECREE THAT DAILY I WALK IN THE SPIRIT THAT THE LIGHT OF CHRIST MAY SHINE BRIGHTLY IN AND THROUGH ME.

I DECLARE AND DECREE THAT YOU HAVE ANOINTED ME WITH THE OIL OF GLADNESS; LET MY MOUTH BE FILLED WITH LAUGHTER AND MY TONGUE WITH SINGING.

I DECLARE AND DECREE THAT ANYTHING THAT IS IN MY LIFE THAT IS ATTRACTING SIN WILL BE EXPOSED AND DESTROYED.

I DECLARE AND DECREE THAT I ADVANCE FROM VICTORY TO VICTORY, TRIUMPH TO TRIUMPH, AND GLORY TO GLORY.

I DECLARE AND DECREE THAT THERE WILL BE NO SUBSTITUTES, NO HOLD UPS, NO SETBACKS, NO DELAYS, AND I WILL RISE TO DO NEW THINGS. I HAVE BEEN ANOINTED FOR IMPACT, IN THE NAME OF JESUS.

I DECLARE AND DECREE THAT SUCCESS AND PROGRESS IS THE WILL OF GOD FOR MY LIFE.

I DECLARE AND DECREE THAT EACH AND EVERY DAY I ADVANCE, I GAIN TERRITORY AND I QUANTUM LEAP INTO MY WEALTHY PLACE.

I DECLARE AND DECREE THAT EVERY PLACE THAT MY FEET TREAD UPON BELONGS TO ME, IN THE NAME OF JESUS.

IN THE NAME OF JESUS THERE IS AN OPEN DOOR OVER MY LIFE IN THE NAME OF JESUS!

I DECLARE AND DECREE THAT THERE IS HEALING AVAILABLE TO ME TODAY IN THE NAME OF JESUS!

HOLY SPIRIT, RELEASE YOUR POWER, RELEASE YOU ANOINTING OVER MY LIFE!

IN THE NAME OF JESUS, HOLY SPIRIT YOU ARE MY STRENGTH, HOLY SPIRIT YOU ARE MY GUIDE!

JESUS YOU ARE THE CENTER OF MY JOY!

HOLY SPIRIT TODAY I SURRENDER ALL TO YOU, I PUT IT IN YOUR HANDS YOU CAN TAKE CARE OF THIS, I SURRENDER ALL!

THERE IS NO FEAR THAT LIVES HERE, WHATEVER THE DEVIL BRINGS TO ME, AROUND ME, I CAN HANDLE IT IN THE NAME OF JESUS! THERE IS NO FEAR HERE! THERE IS NO FEAR HERE!

I CHOOSE TO FOLLOW YOU HOLY SPIRIT IT IS MY CHOICE, I CHOOSE TO FOLLOW YOU!

THE VOICE OF THE STRANGER I WILL NOT FOLLOW!

SIN HAS NO POWER, NO AUTHORITY OVER ME IN THE NAME OF JESUS!

IN THE NAME OF JESUS, ANYONE THAT HURT ME TODAY I CHOOSE TO FORGIVE THEM!

THE ENEMY HAS NO POWER, NO AUTHORITY OVER MY LIFE IN THE NAME OF JESUS. I SURRENDER ALL TO GOD IN THE NAME OF JESUS!

THANK YOU LORD THAT EVERY NEGATIVE THING THAT COMES MY WAY, YOU WOULD CHANGE IT AND TURN IT AROUND FOR MY GOOD AND FOR YOUR GLORY IN THE NAME OF JESUS!

I RELEASE THAT AND DECLARE IT OVER MY LIFE IN JESUS NAME AMEN!

WE DECLARE AND DECREE THAT WE WILL NOT SUFFER INSTABILITY THIS YEAR BUT WE WILL EXCELL IN ALL AREAS ACCORDING TO YOUR WILL FOR US

WE DECLARE AND DECREE THAT OUR BODIES WILL NOT BE A HABITATION FOR SICKNESS AND DISEASE BUT IT WILL REMAIN A TEMPLE OF THE MOST HIGH GOD.

WE DECLARE AND DECREE THAT OUR FEET WILL BE GUARDED, STRENGTHENED AND ANOINTED FOR SPEED THROUGHOUT THE REST OF THE YEAR

WE DECLARE AND DECREE THAT WE SHALL BE PEOPLE OF BIG THINGS, AND THE LORD WILL BLESS US WITH UNSURPASSED WISDOM

WE DECLARE AND DECREE THAT WE HAVE A GOD GIVEN GRACE TO ADOPT THE RIGHT STRATEGY FOR EVERY SITUATION AND TO BE AT THE RIGHT PLACE AT THE RIGHT TIME ALL THE TIME.

I DECLARE AND DECREE THAT MY CHILD/CHILDREN ARE BLESSED AND HIGHLY FAVORED.

I DECLARE AND DECREE THAT MY CHILD/CHILDREN ARE TAUGHT OF THE LORD AND THE WORD THAT IS HIDDEN IN THEIR HEART WILL PROCEED OUT OF THEIR MOUTHS.

I DECLARE AND DECREE THAT MY CHILD/CHILDREN HAVE THE MIND OF CHRIST AND THE WISDOM OF GOD IS MADE IN THEM.

I DECLARE AND DECREE THAT MY CHILD/CHILDREN DO NOT ENTANGLE THEMSELVES IN THE CARES OF THE WORLD BUT THAT THEY SEEK GOD, HIS KINGDOM AND HIS RIGHTEOUSNESS THAT ALL THINGS MAY BE ADDED ON TO THEM.

I DECLARE AND DECREE THAT MY CHILD/CHILDREN WALK IN HEALTH AND HEALING ALL THE DAYS OF THEIR LIVES.

I DECLARE AND DECREE THAT MY CHILD/CHILDREN ARE COVERED AND PROTECTED BY THE SPIRIT OF GOD AND HIS ANGELS FORM WALLS OF PROTECTION AROUND THEM.

DAILY POWER DECLARATIONS

I DECLARE AND DECREE THAT MY CHILD/CHILDREN ARE SUBMITTED AND OBEDIENT TO YOU LORD, TO US AND TO THE AUTHORITIES THAT YOU HAVE PLACED OVER THEM. GREAT IS THE PEACE OF MY CHILDREN.

I DECLARE I AM A VICTORIOUS BELIEVER.

I DECLARE THAT I AM BLOOD BOUGHT AND A HOLY GHOST FILLED BELIEVER.

I DECLARE THAT I AM THE RIGHTEOUSNESS OF GOD IN CHRIST JESUS.

I DECLARE THAT INCREASE COMES FROM THE NORTH, THE SOUTH, THE EAST AND THE WEST.

I DECLARE THAT I WALK BY FAITH AND NOT BY SIGHT.

I DECLARE THAT THE WILL OF GOD WILL BE DONE IN MY LIFE.

I DECLARE THAT I HAVE NO FEAR BUT THAT THE PEACE OF GOD RESTS OVER MY LIFE, IN THE NAME OF JESUS.

I WALK BY FAITH AND NOT BY SIGHT.

HOLY SPIRIT, DWELL IN ME, WORK IN ME, AND MINISTER TO ME TODAY.

I DECLARE THAT EVERY OPEN DOOR OF THE ENEMY TO MY LIFE IS CLOSED, IN THE NAME OF JESUS.

I DECLARE THAT EVERY GENERATIONAL CURSE PLACED OVER MY LIFE IS BROKEN, AND I SEND IT BACK TO HELL FROM WHERE IT CAME, IN THE NAME OF JESUS.

I DECLARE THAT I AM FREE FROM EVERY DEMONIC SPIRIT THAT WOULD ATTACH ITSELF TO MY LIFE, IN THE NAME OF JESUS.

I DECLARE THAT MY LIFE IS FREE FROM ALL GENERATIONAL, ANCESTRAL, FAMILIAL AND INHERITED SIN, INIQUITY, AND TRANGRESSIONS.

I DECLARE THAT I AM FORGIVEN, RESTORED, DELIVERED, AND ANOINTED TO MOVE FORWARD, UPWARD, AND ONWARD IN EVERY AREA OF MY LIFE, IN THE NAME OF JESUS.

I DECLARE AND DECREE THAT I SEE THROUGH EVERY LIE OF THE ENEMY, AND I KNOW ABUNDANCE IS A BIRTHRIGHT THAT I HAVE.

I DECLARE AND DECREE MY CAREER IS OVERFLOWING WITH KINGDOM SUCCESS.

I DECLARE AND DECREE THAT ANGELS ARE ASCENDING AND DESCENDING OVER MY LIFE WITH

BOUNTIFUL BLESSINGS.

I DECLARE AND DECREE THAT I AM WALKING THROUGH DOORS OF OPPORTUNITY THAT HAVE BEEN AWAITING MY ARRIVAL.

I DECLARE AND DECREE THAT ALL SITUATIONS ARE WORKING OUT, LOOSE ENDS ARE BEING TIED UP, AND ALL THINGS ARE WORKING FOR ME.

I DECLARE AND DECREE THAT I RISE ABOVE EVERY NEGATIVE SITUATION, I HAVE HINDS FEET TO LEAP OVER WALLS OF HINDRANCES, AND I STAND ON TOP WITH ALL THINGS UNDER MY FEET.

I DECLARE AND DECREE THAT FORWARD THINKING, FORWARD MOVING, AND DILIGENT LIVING ARE CREATING GOOD SUCCESS FOR ME, IN THE NAME OF JESUS.

I DECLARE AND DECREE THAT IN THE NAME OF JESUS EVERY NEGATIVE AND DESTRUCTIVE HABIT I CONSIDER POWERLESS TO PRODUCE ANY NEGATIVE EFFECTS AGAINST ME.

I DECLARE AND DECREE THAT EVERY NEGATIVE HABIT AND ADDICTION IS BROKEN OFF OF MY LIFE BY

THE POWER OF THE BLOOD OF JESUS FROM THE CROWN OF MY HEAD TO THE SOLES OF MY FEET. I THANK YOU THAT YOUR POWER IS AVAILABLE TO ME, IN THE NAME OF JESUS.

I DECLARE AND DECREE THAT THERE IS AN OPEN DOOR OVER MY LIFE, IN THE NAME OF JESUS.

I DECLARE AND DECREE THAT YOUR HEALING ANOINTING IS ABLE TO REVERSE SICKNESS AND DISEASE OVER MY LIFE.

I DECLARE AND DECREE, HOLY SPIRIT, I RELEASE YOUR POWER AND ANOINTING OVER MY LIFE, IN THE NAME OF JESUS.

I DECLARE AND DECREE, HOLY SPIRIT, YOU ARE MY STRENGTH AND YOU ARE MY GUIDE.

I DECLARE AND DECREE, JESUS, YOU ARE THE CENTER OF MY JOY; THERE IS NO FEAR THAT LIVES IN HERE.

I DECLARE AND DECREE THAT I DWELL IN THE SECRET PLACE OF THE MOST HIGH AND MY FAMILY AND I ARE SAFE.

I DECLARE AND DECREE THAT I AM ARMED AND

DANGEROUS.

I DECLARE AND DECREE THAT THE LORD IS MY BANNER AND HE SHALL FIGHT MY BATTLES.

I DECLARE AND DECREE THAT THERE IS NO LACK IN MY HOUSE, FOR MY GOD SHALL SUPPLY ALL MY NEEDS.

I DECLARE AND DECREE THAT JESUS IS MY ROCK, MY REFUGE, AND MY FORTRESS.

I DECLARE AND DECREE THAT MY GOD IS ABLE TO DO EXCEEDINGLY ABUNDANTLY ABOVE ALL THAT I COULD EVER ASK OR THINK IN EVERY AREA OF MY LIFE.

I DECLARE AND DECREE THAT I SERVE THE GOD OF MORE THAN ENOUGH; THE LORD IS MY PORTION.

I DECLARE AND DECREE THAT THE SPIRIT OF CONDEMNATION HAS BEEN BROKEN OFF OF MY LIFE.

I DECLARE AND DECREE THANK YOU, LORD, FOR SENDING YOUR SON, JESUS CHRIST.

I DECLARE AND DECREE THAT I DO NOT RECEIVE THE SPIRIT OF DEATH BUT I RECEIVE LIFE AND ETERNAL LIFE.

I DECLARE AND DECREE THAT I HATE EVIL AND

EMBRACE LIFE; I EMBRACE YOU LORD AND YOUR WORD.

I DECLARE AND DECREE THAT THE HOLY SPIRIT INCREASE IN ME, AND I DECREASE SELF, SINS, AND STRONGHOLDS. I RELEASE YOU, HOLY SPIRIT, TO DO YOUR WORK IN ME.

I DECLARE AND DECREE THAT I WALK IN YOUR WORD THAT MY JOY MAY BE FULL.

I DECLARE AND DECREE THAT MY LIFE IS IN ALIGNMENT WITH YOUR WILL AND YOUR WORD AND I WILL SEE THE BLESSINGS OF THE LORD MANIFESTED IN MY LIFE.

I DECLARE AND DECREE IN THE REMAINDER OF THIS YEAR I SHALL BE A CANDIDATE FOR UNCOMMON FAVOR AND BLESSING.

I DECLARE AND DECREE PROMOTION AND ELEVATION SHALL FIND ME OVER AND OVER AGAIN.

I DECLARE AND DECREE GOD SHALL TURN MY WORST TIMES INTO MY BEST TIMES.

I DECLARE AND DECREE MY GOD SHALL ARISE THIS

YEAR AND MY ENEMIES SHALL BE SCATTERED, IN JESUS NAME.

I DECLARE AND DECREE THAT THIS WEEK IS MY WEEK FOR BREAKTHROUGHS AND IT IS MY WEEK OF FAVOR.

I DECLARE AND DECREE THIS MONTH WILL BE A MONTH OF UNCOMMON BLESSINGS, PROVISIONS, AND OPPORTUNITIES.

I DECLARE AND DECREE THAT THIS IS MY SET TIME, THIS IS MY SEASON, AND I WILL WALK IN MY DUE SEASON, IN JESUS NAME.

I DECLARE AND DECREE NO MATTER WHAT HAPPENS IN THIS WORLD, I WILL ALWAYS PROSPER.

I DECLARE AND DECREE NO MATTER WHAT SITUATIONS I FACE, I WILL OVERCOME THEM ALL.

I DECLARE AND DECREE NO MATTER WHAT THE OBSTACLES ARE, I WILL RISE ABOVE THEM ALL.

I DECLARE AND DECREE NO MATTER WHAT TRIALS OR TESTS ARE BEFORE ME, I WILL PRESS FORWARD.

I DECLARE AND DECREE NO MATTER WHAT

HINDRANCE THAT I COME UP AGAINST, I WILL MOVE FORWARD IN MY POWER AND AUTHORITY.

I DECLARE AND DECREE NO MATTER WHAT TRIBULATIONS COME MY WAY, I WILL NOT FEAR FOR YOU ARE WITH ME AND YOU GO BEFORE ME, IN THE NAME OF JESUS.

I DECLARE AND DECREE THAT I HAVE THE VICTORY TODAY.

I DECLARE AND DECREE THAT I AM A CARRIER OF THE ANOINTING.

I DECLARE AND DECREE THAT I SEE AND RECEIVE MY VICTORY.

I SHOUT WITH THE SHOUT OF TRIUMPH FOR MY MIRACLE.

I DECLARE AND DECREE THAT I SEE THE WALLS COMING DOWN, IN THE NAME OF JESUS.

I DECLARE AND DECREE THAT I WALK IN THE MIRACULOUS.

I DECLARE AND DECREE THAT THE FIGHTER WITHIN

ME RISES AND TAKES BY FORCE THOSE THINGS THAT BELONG TO ME.

I DECLARE AND DECREE I AM BLESSED, I AM HEALTHY, AND I AM PRODUCTIVE, IN THE NAME OF JESUS.

I DECLARE AND DECREE I AM SAVED, SANCTIFIED AND DELIVERED FROM EVERY DEMONIC HOLD IN MY LIFE, IN THE NAME OF JESUS.

I DECLARE AND DECREE MY PURPOSE IS IN CHRIST, MY IDENTIFICATION IS IN CHRIST, AND MY FUTURE IS IN CHRIST.

I DECLARE AND DECREE I SPEAK TO THE MOUNTAIN AND THE MOUNTAIN MUST BE MOVED, IN THE NAME OF JESUS.

I DECLARE AND DECREE WHAT THE ENEMY HAS STOLEN HE MUST RETURN SEVENFOLD AND MY HOUSEHOLD IS BLESSED, IN THE NAME OF JESUS.

I DECLARE AND DECREE THAT I WILL NOT LOOK BACK NOR TURN BACK BUT I WILL MOVE FORWARD, IN THE NAME OF JESUS.

I DECLARE AND DECREE THAT SOMETHING GOOD IS COMING TO ME TODAY, IN THE NAME OF JESUS.

I DECLARE AND DECREE THAT THE HAND OF THE LORD IS ON ME STRONGLY TODAY.

I DECLARE AND DECREE I WILL LIVE AND NOT DIE AND DECLARE THE WORKS OF THE LORD.

I DECLARE AND DECREE THAT TODAY IS MY DAY; TODAY I WIN.

I DECLARE AND DECREE THAT TODAY MY LIFE IS IN THE HAND OF GOD, AND HIS MERCY AND GOODNESS WILL FOLLOW ME.

I DECLARE AND DECREE THAT EVERYTHING THAT MY HANDS TOUCH TURNS TO GOLD, IN THE NAME OF JESUS.

I DECLARE AND DECREE THAT MY CHILDREN AND I INCREASE MORE AND MORE.

I DECLARE AND DECREE THAT THE PEACE OF GOD, THE JOY THAT IS UNSPEAKABLE AND FULL OF GLORY, AND HIS UNCONDITIONAL LOVE REST OVER MY LIFE, IN THE NAME OF JESUS.

I DECLARE AND DECREE THAT THE PRESENCE OF GOD FOLLOWS ME WHEREVER I GO.

I DECLARE AND DECREE I HAVE THE PROSPERITY OF GOD ON THE INSIDE OF ME.

DAILY POWER DECLARATIONS

I DECLARE AND DECREE I HAVE THE POWER OF GOD ON THE INSIDE OF ME.

I DECLARE AND DECREE I HAVE THE PROMISE OF THE HOLY SPIRIT.

I DECLARE AND DECREE I HAVE THE PLANS OF GOD FOR ME TODAY, THAT HE WILL SHOW ME WHERE TO GO AND HOW TO GO.

I DECLARE AND DECREE THAT GOD IS ABLE TO KEEP ME FROM FALLING, AND HE PRESENTS ME FAULTLESS, IN THE NAME OF JESUS.

I DECLARE AND DECREE THAT I HAVE THE ASSURANCE THAT MY DESTINY IS SEALED BY THE HOLY SPIRIT.

I DECLARE AND I DECREE THAT I AM TRANSFORMED INTO AN AGENT OF GOD.

I DECLARE AND I DECREE THAT I HAVE NO TIME FOR LAZINESS OR SICKNESS AND ALL CURSES ARE BROKEN OFF OF MY LIFE.

I DECLARE AND I DECREE I WILL NOT FAIL AND I WILL SUCCEED; IT IS MY TURN AROUND DAY.

I DECLARE AND I DECREE THAT I AM AN AMBASSADOR OF GOD AND ALL DIPLOMATIC RIGHTS AND PRIVILEDGES ARE EXTENDED TO ME.

I DECLARE AND I DECREE THAT I HAVE BEEN CHOSEN, EQUIPPED, AND EMPOWERED TO DO MIGHTY THINGS IN THIS WORLD.

I DECLARE AND I DECREE THAT I AM UNITED TO CHRIST AND I BEAR GOOD FRUIT IN ALL THAT I DO.

I DECLARE AND I DECREE THAT DAILY I WALK WITH PURPOSE AND SINGLENESS OF MIND TO BE VICTORIOUS.

I DECLARE AND DECREE THAT I WELCOME YOUR PEACE IN MY LIFE, FATHER.

I DECLARE AND DECREE THAT I WILL NOT WORRY, I WILL NOT DOUBT, BUT I WILL BELIIEVE YOUR WORD.

I DECLARE AND DECREE THAT I CHOOSE TO FORGIVE TODAY AND LET GO OF EVERY NEGATIVE THOUGHT.

I DECLARE AND DECREE THAT I CHOOSE TO LOVE YOU, HONOR YOU, AND BRING GLORY TO YOUR NAME IN ALL THAT I DO.

I DECLARE AND DECREE THAT, FATHER, TODAY, I

CHOOSE TO WORSHIP YOU IN SPIRIT AND IN TRUTH, IN THE NAME JESUS.

I DECLARE AND DECREE THAT NOW THERE IS NO CONDEMNATION ON ME BECAUSE I BELONG TO CHRIST.

I DECLARE AND DECREE THAT I AM REDEEMED, JUSTIFIED, AND SET FREE FROM THE BONDAGE OF SIN, IN THE NAME OF JESUS.

I DECLARE AND DECREE THAT IN THE NAME OF JESUS, GOD, I TRUST YOU TODAY; I WILL NOT MAKE ANY DECISIONS TODAY WITHOUT YOU.

I DECLARE AND DECREE THAT ALL MY DECISIONS WILL BE MADE AFTER SEEKING YOUR FACE.

I DECLARE AND DECREE THAT I LET GO AND I SURRENDER TO YOUR WILL AND TO YOUR WAY.

I DECLARE AND DECREE THAT YOU DIRECT MY PATH, FOR I PUT MY TRUST TOTALLY AND COMPLETELY IN YOU.

I DECLARE AND DECREE THAT YOU LEAD ME AND GUIDE ME, AND I KNOW THAT YOU WILL BRING ME TO MY EXPECTED END.

I DECLARE AND DECREE THAT YOU ARE MY WISDOM IN EVERY SITUATION; THEREFORE, I DO NOT MAKE ANY DECISIONS IN HASTE.

I DECLARE AND DECREE THAT I HEAR YOUR VOICE AND I FOLLOW YOU WHEREVER YOU LEAD ME.

I DECLARE AND DECREE THAT I AM A PRISONER OF THE LORD AND I WALK IN THE VOCATION TO WHICH I HAVE BEEN CALLED, IN THE NAME OF JESUS.

I DECLARE AND DECREE THAT I BEAR UP MY BROTHERS' AND SISTERS' FAULTS IN LOVE, AND THE BOND OF PEACE RESTS, RULES, AND ABIDES ON THE INSIDE OF ME.

I DECLARE AND DECREE THAT GOD HAS GIVEN ME GRACE ACCORDING TO THE MEASURE AND THE GIFT OF CHRIST.

I DECLARE AND DECREE THAT I HAVE RECEIVED THE FIVE FOLD MINISTRY THAT I MAY BE EQUIPPED AND PERFECTED IN THE THINGS OF GOD, IN THE NAME OF JESUS.

I DECLARE AND DECREE THAT I AM ANOINTED TO DO GREAT WORKS.

DAILY POWER DECLARATIONS

I DECLARE AND DECREE THAT MY LIFE IS LED BY THE SPIRIT OF GOD AND ALL MY LIFE IS ALIGNED WITH THE WORD OF GOD.

I DECLARE AND DECREE THAT I AM A SERVANT OF RIGHTEOUSNESS AND I AM NO LONGER A SLAVE TO SIN.

I DECLARE AND DECREE THAT THE BLESSINGS OF GOD REST ON MY LIFE AND GOD'S LOVE, PEACE, AND JOY FLOW IN AND THROUGH ME, IN THE NAME OF JESUS.

I DECLARE AND DECREE THAT TODAY I WILL LEAD MANY SOULS INTO THE KINGDOM OF GOD BY THE ANOINTING OF THE HOLY SPIRIT.

I DECLARE AND DECREE THAT MY WORDS WILL BRING ENCOURAGEMENT AND WISDOM TO THOSE AROUND ME.

I DECLARE AND DECREE THAT MY ACTIONS WILL SPEAK AND REFLECT MY RELATIONSHIP WITH CHRIST.

I DECLARE AND DECREE THAT MY FAMILY IS COVERED AND PROTECTED BY GOD WHEREVER THEY GO.

I DECLARE AND DECREE THAT MY CHILDREN ARE HIGHLY FAVORED OF GOD AND THEY OPERATE WITH

A SPIRIT OF EXCELLENCE.

I DECLARE AND DECREE THAT AS FOR ME AND MY HOUSE, WE WILL SERVE THE LORD.

I DECLARE AND DECREE THAT I WILL ACCOMPLISH MY ASSIGNMENT IN CHRIST.

I DECLARE AND DECREE THAT MY FINANCIAL SITUATION IS IMPROVING EVERY DAY.

I DECLARE AND DECREE THAT I HAVE AN ATTITUDE OF GRATITUDE.

I DECLARE AND DECREE THAT THE HOLY SPIRIT GIVES ME A HEART OF INTEGRITY.

I DECLARE AND DECREE THAT GOD'S PLAN AND MISSION FOR MY LIFE WILL COME TO PASS AND NOTHING WILL STOP IT. I WILL FULFILL GOD'S DESTINY FOR MY LIFE.

I DECLARE AND DECREE THAT MY MISSION AND VISION THAT GOD GAVE TO ME WILL BE FULFILLED. IN THE NAME OF JESUS.

I DECLARE AND DECREE THAT FOOTSTEPS ARE

ORDERED, MY HANDS ARE DILIGENT. AND I AM WELL ABLE TO DO THIS LABOR OF LOVE.

I DECLARE AND DECREE THAT I LOVE WISDOM AND I EMBRACE IT.

I DECLARE AND DECREE THAT I AM ESTABLISHED IN THE RIGHTEOUSNESS OF GOD.

I DECLARE AND DECREE THAT I HAVE A THIRST FOR RIGHTEOUSNESS AND THE KINGDOM OF GOD.

I DECLARE AND DECREE THAT I RECEIVE GOD'S ROD AND HIS REPROOF, FOR THEY RELEASE THE WISDOM OF GOD IN ME, IN THE NAME OF JESUS.

I DECLARE AND DECREE THAT I HAVE A DEEP DESIRE TO BE IN THE PRESENCE, FOR IT IS THE PLACE OF DELIGHT AND PLEASURE.

I DECLARE AND DECREE THAT I LOVE THE WORD OF THE LORD AND I DAILY HIDE IT DEEP IN MY HEART.

I DECLARE AND DECREE THAT I RECOGNIZE THE HAND OF GOD IN MY LIFE AND I KNOW THAT GOD IS ALWAYS WITH ME, IN THE NAME OF JESUS.

I DECLARE AND DECREE THAT THERE IS NO BARREN AREA IN MY LIFE.

I DECLARE AND DECREE THAT MY COAST IS ENLARGED AND MY TERRITORY IS ENLARGED BY THE LORD JESUS CHRIST.

I DECLARE AND DECREE THAT I AM BREAKING LOOSE WITH PROPSERITY ON THE LEFT AND THE RIGHT.

I DECLARE AND DECREE THAT I WALK BY FAITH AND I DO NOT WALK IN FEAR, IN THE NAME OF JESUS.

I DECLARE AND DECREE THAT I HAVE BEEN REDEEMED FROM THE HAND OF THE ENEMY.

I DECLARE AND DECREE THAT THAT I HAVE BEEN JUSTIFIED BY FAITH IN CHRIST.

I DECLARE AND DECREE THAT I AM FREE AND WHOM THE SON SETS FREE IS FREE INDEED.

I DECLARE AND DECREE THAT I AM A PRISONER OF HOPE.

I DECLARE AND DECREE THAT I HAVE FORSAKEN MY UNRIGHTEOUS THOUGHTS AND I HAVE EMBRACED THE THOUGHTS OF GOD.

DAILY POWER DECLARATIONS

I DECLARE AND DECREE THAT I AM THE LENDER AND NOT THE BORROWER.

I DECLARE AND DECREE THAT I WALK IN DIVINE PROSPERITY EVERY DAY OF MY LIFE, IN THE NAME OF JESUS.

I DECLARE AND DECREE THAT I AM THE HEAD AND NOT THE TAIL.

I DECLARE AND DECREE TODAY IS A DAY OF UNCOMMON BLESSINGS FOR MY LIFE, IN THE NAME OF JESUS.

I DECLARE AND DECREE THAT MY LOVED ONES ARE PARTAKERS OF THE OVERFLOW IN MY LIFE.

I DECLARE AND DECREE THAT I HAVE ALREADY WON IN THE SPIRIT.

I DECLARE AND DECREE THAT MY POTENTIAL IS LIMITLESS IN CHRIST.

I DECLARE AND DECREE THAT THE HOLY SPIRIT RELEASE WHAT BELONGS TO ME THIS YEAR, IN THE NAME OF JESUS.

I DECLARE AND DECREE THAT I WILL NOT LOOK BACK BUT I AM LOOKING FORWARD, IN THE NAME OF JESUS.

I DECLARE AND DECREE THAT YOUR WISDOM AND FAVOR ARE RELEASED OVER ME TODAY.

I DECLARE AND DECREE THAT I HAVE THE MIND OF CHRIST AND I LIVE BY FAITH.

I DECLARE AND DECREE THAT I AM AN OVERCOMER AND I LIVE ACCORDING TO GOD'S WILL FOR MY LIFE.

I DECLARE AND DECREE THAT I WILL NOT MOVE ACCORDING TO THE PAST BUT I WILL MOVE FORWARD.

I DECLARE AND DECREE THAT I HAVE BEEN REDEEMED FROM SIN, AND SIN HAS NO POWER OVER MY LIFE.

I DECLARE AND DECREE THAT THE LORD HAS NOT REMOVED HIS COVENANT PEACE; I HAVE THE COVENANT OF PEACE.

I DECLARE AND DECREE THAT ALL MY CHILDREN WILL BE TAUGHT OF THE LORD, AND GREAT IS THE PEACE OF MY CHILREN.

I DECLARE AND DECREE THAT I AM ESTABLISHED IN RIGHTEOUSNESS AND I AM FAR FROM OPPRESSION AND FEAR WHICH CANNOT COME NEAR ME, IN THE NAME OF JESUS.

I DECLARE AND DECREE THAT WHOEVER GATHERS AGAINST ME SHALL FALL FOR GOD'S SAKE.

I DECLARE AND DECREE THAT I AGREE WITH THE WORD OF GOD CONCERNING MY LIFE AND IT WILL BE ACCOMPLISHED.

CONTACT US

Speak The Word Ministries
7 Peter's Rest,
Christiansted, St. Croix
USVI 00823
(340) 778-1575
Email us at pastor@stwmi.com

Join Us

START YOUR DAY RIGHT IN PRAYER

1-407-308-0002

Weekdays 6:30am to 6:45am AST

www.stwmi.com

ABOUT DEXTER SKEPPLE

There is a relatively small segment of leaders in the business world; individuals who seem able to build relationships, trust, and rapport with almost anyone, and then are able to maintain the relationships and make connections between people, creating partnerships and alliances, and motivating forward momentum to 'get things done.'

Dexter Skepple is one of those people, and 'getting things done' and driving results—through collaboration, partnerships, and relationships—is what he is all about. With an enthusiastic and genuinely friendly attitude, Mr. Skepple radiates a sincere passion for delivering value and benefits to everyone with whom he comes in contact.

A Pilot by training, Dexter Skepple earned his Bachelor of Science degree from the University of Central Texas, (now Texas A&M) in 1993. After spending five years as a full-time professional pilot, he made a life-changing decision that he could have a larger, positive impact on more people if he moved into full-time ministry. After starting Speak the Word Ministries on St. Croix in 1998, the ministry quickly accelerated and has been in existence for 20 years. He is the founder of "Start Your Day Right Prayer In Prayer." Recently he started an Orphanage in the Dominican Republic "Mansion of Hope." Mr. Skepple also conducts marriage seminars throughout the Caribbean, He has been successfully married for over 25 years to his lovely wife, Terry.

Mr. Skepple has always had a passion for seeing men succeed. Whether young or old, he has poured endless amounts of his time and resources into mentoring, counseling and motivating men to reach their full potential. Born and raised on St. Croix, he saw a need for direction, purpose and discipline in the lives of our men. In 2003, he launched the Boys to Men/Save Our Sons program—a non-profit, program designed to focus on building long-lasting, loyal relationships between adult mentors and the young men of the St. Croix community. It has been an exceptional program with many success stories.

A professional Pilot for over twenty-five years, Dexter Skepple is presently the President of a small charter company "Capitol Air" located in St. Thomas, U.S.V.I. Throughout his life, he has repeatedly proved his ability to lead through diverse and challenging situations. As a Pastor, Administrator, Entrepreneur and Advocate for family, he is an excellent agent of change and has a documented track record of accomplishments that include the turnaround of chaotic and struggling operations; start-up and management of a thriving non-denominational ministry; and creation and launch of a landmark mentoring program for young men.

Today, Mr. Skepple resides on St. Croix, where his ministry is located, with his family. As he has top-notch qualifications working within our community, it is challenging to put his skills in a "box." But what is absolutely clear is that he adds a great deal of value to any environment where he is placed.

Made in the USA
Middletown, DE
15 November 2021